Cyrus C Camp

Labor, capital and money

their just relations

Cyrus C Camp

Labor, capital and money
their just relations

ISBN/EAN: 9783744741668

Printed in Europe, USA, Canada, Australia, Japan

Cover: Foto ©Suzi / pixelio.de

More available books at **www.hansebooks.com**

LABOR, CAPITAL AND MONEY;

THEIR JUST RELATIONS.

AN EXPOSITION OF ECONOMIC ERROR WHICH PERVERTS PUBLIC
SENTIMENT, CONTROLS LEGISLATION, BARS JUST ENACT-
MENTS, PRODUCES NEEDLESS STRIFE BETWEEN LABOR
AND CAPITAL, IDLENESS AND POVERTY AMID ABUN-
DANCE, CAUSES UNJUST DISTRIBUTION OF WEALTH,
BUSINESS DEPRESSIONS AND PANICS, AND SAPS
THE FOUNDATION OF ALL GOVERNMENT.

BY

C. C. CAMP.

This inquiry discloses the fact that "Ricardo's Law of Rent" (so called) is
founded in error, and consequently overthrows all theories and conclusions
based upon it.

BRADFORD, PA.:
PRESS OF D. W. LERCH, PUBLISHER.
1888.

PREFACE.

This work is the outgrowth of a presentiment of the coming of the industrial struggle which now forces itself upon the attention of society. For years there has grown upon me the conviction that an unseen evil influence was gathering a pressure and power, which, sweeping in a great cycle, would sooner or later engulf civilization, unless discovered and eradicated. I determined to sift political economy to the bottom in order to aid, if possible, in the accomplishment of this object. In this investigation I found radical errors in the groundwork, and from thence pervading every part of political science, as previously promulgated. By correcting these errors I have laid up one stone of truth upon another, not heeding where the truth might lead, until in a complete explanation of existing conditions it is presented to the reader. The result is as much a surprise to me as it can be to any other person.

The practical overthrow of the law of rent, hitherto considered as firmly established as the

law of gravitation, and the consequent ellimina-
tion of its influence from the contemplation of
the conditions of mankind, which have hitherto
been regarded as sequential penalties of its
operation, is a result as gratifying as it is
novel.

That opportunities and facilities are found to
exist, which can be made to supply abundantly
every necessity, or rational want of man, as well
as means to secure a just and equitable distribution without any shock or unnecessary suffering
in society, is especially pleasing to me.

That the work may assist in upbuilding truth,
in establishing justice and fraternity, in maintaining peace and plenty, as a means of securing
happiness to all is the wish of

THE AUTHOR.

FREDONIA, N. Y., August 1, 1887.

TABLE OF CONTENTS.

INTRODUCTION.

Conditions of society which challenge investigation.

The nineteenth century has witnessed the
most remarkable awakening of mental and physical activity. Patient, earnest, fearless investi-
gators in every department of science, have
invaded the domain of nature in search of principles and facts which might add to the welfare
and happiness of mankind.

What science has demonstrated, the practical
mind has utilized. The busy-brained inventor,
has subdued the subtle and potent forces
of nature, and made them subject of his will;
has compassed land and sea with devices to
facilitate commercial intercourse; has multiplied
and remultiplied the efficiency of labor, until
productive power and production itself, has
passed the utmost bounds of necessity, of desire
or caprice.

The student of political science has dug to the
root of social relations; has boldly challenged

the right of ancient superstitions and usurpations to cast their shadows across the present; has unfolded the rights of individual humanity, and claims to have demonstrated that the object of government founded in justice and bounded by equity can only be attained by securing to the individual citizen the greatest liberty and happiness consistent with public good.

Were these deductions true, and governments founded upon such principles amidst abundance of production, it would seem to follow as a necessary consequence that poverty would be eradicated and want and wretchedness unknown.

The most casual observation shows that no such results have been attained. Go where you will in civilized society and the poor are always with you. Amidst abundance of wealth which his own hand has created; amidst graineries full to repletion; amidst warehouses of fabrics, whose texture bespeaks warmth, comfort and health; amidst luxuries limited only by satiety, the laborer stands compelled to beg permission to share sufficient to satisfy a niggardly necessity. The place where brightness and revelry and mirth hold perpetual holiday, casts its shadow over the hovel, where the deeper shadow of want and wretchedness is never absent.

The laboring many, trudging to their ceaseless treadmill of half requitted toil, behold the rich few in gay attire and gaudy trappings, go jauntily to resorts of pleasure, feeling that every farthing of useless waste represents comforts and wants of wife or child taken out of their labor, they know not how or why.

The clod falls continually upon the coffin of him who died from surfeit; and, if we listen closely, we can ever hear the hearse driver, on his way to the Potter's field, singing:

"Rattle his bones over the stones,
  He's only a pauper whom nobody owns."

Nor do we find this condition confined to wage workers alone. Everywhere in society, thrifty, industrious and energetic producers, toil as they will, husband their capital as they may, yet life presents no rest or leisure, no opportunity for culture—simply a struggle for bare existence.

The manufacturer, in the tide of prosperity, finds his storehouses filling with goods. He finds warehouses crowded everywhere. One by one, competent, faithful hands are discharged. Business comes to a standstill. We call it a "business depression." For want of knowledge of the cause, one says, "Over production"; and another, with just as little reason, says, "Want of consumption."

Over production, indeed! When you can almost hear the rustle of the angel's wings that bore away the breath of a child who died for want of breath; and ever and anon come whirlwinds, we call them panics, when capital struggles no longer and mills and factories stand idle; and he who but yesterday was weaving garlands of happiness in a thousand hearts finds himself stranded and none "so poor to do him reverence."

The question of questions which this generation has to answer is, "Why, amid abundance, poverty remains?" What are the means by which production is taken from the large body of producers and concentrated in the hands of a few?

The time has passed for evasion or subterfuge. Ridicule and sarcasm must give place to reason. Thinking men are looking each other in the face and asking, "What of the night?"

That no one of the current explanations finds lodgment in the judgment of men is evident from the painful uncertainty and doubt in master minds, and the apathy of those who could and would correct existing evils, if a sure and steady light were thrown upon this subject.

One claims that tariff is the cause, another that tariff is the remedy; one that a tax upon land is too grievious to be borne, another that tax is the remedy, and so on to the end; while, as a result of confusion, organized labor and organized capital stand confronting each other like hostile foes in armed neutrality, when by every truth of science, every principle of justice, every teaching of political economy, it can be demonstrated that labor and capital are identical in interest, identical in the great struggle for industrial emancipation, identical in success, indentical in defeat.

That these conditions are not the result of natural laws is evident by the fact that the laborer, whether working for himself or another, produces more than enough to supply all his necessities and even the luxuries of life. This would be retained by him in the natural order of things did not the greater portion, by some power supreme and incomprehensible, slip from his grasp.

If not natural, it is in the power of just government to correct.

Lurking somewhere in social or political

adjustment, must be found an explanation of these anomalous conditions, which has escaped previous writers upon this subject.

I propose to sift out the error which obscures all previous reasoning upon these questions; to explain, by a strict application to the rules of political science, the causes which lead to existing unjust conditions and point out a broad, clear way to the equitable distribution of wealth.

I shall hew to the line. If I cut through knotty superstitions or prejudices, I can only answer, my duty is to mankind and not to any man or set of men.

ERRATA.

Page   7, line 6, "purchaser" should read producer.
"   17, "   13, "not production" "   not productive
"   81, "   24, "one-tenth" should read seven-tenths
"   149, "   14, "a little over" "   a little less than.
"   184, Transpose lines 14 and 15.
"   185, "influx should read flux.

BOOK I.

Of the Production of Wealth.

CHAPTER I.

Definition of words used in economic writings, showing the distinction between land, labor and capital as the factions of production and money the factor of distribution.

The object of this work is to ascertain the causes which lead to extreme poverty and extreme wealth in every stage of civilization; or in other words, to ascertain by what means a small portion of society absorb the products of labor, except the bare living of the purchaser; to show that this condition is not natural or just and to suggest a remedy.

To accomplish this it will be necessary to examine and explain so much of political economy as relates to the production of wealth; to ascertain the factors of production, their relations, mode of development and contributions to final results, and afterwards to note the distribution of the product, through the various channels, in which it is caused to flow, by natural and artificial laws controling civilized society.

In this examination the technical terms of political economy will constantly recur. Here trouble begins. The nomenclature of this science is not accurate.

Those accounted the foremost writers on economic subjects use the same terms to express different ideas, to express diverse ideas, and sometimes ideas of opposition. Besides this, the technical use is often much more extended or restricted than the common and vulgar use of the same word. Now, as I desire to make this work a demonstration as accurate and conclusive as a theorem of Euclid, and as I also desire to make it useful to that large class of society who have little opportunity to follow economic pursuits, I propose to define such terms as I use with scientific accuracy, and also to explain when the ordinary use expands or contracts their meaning. This does not require any new terms, but simply the use of the most familiar and common words confined to one meaning, and thus stripped of their usual source of ambiguity.

It is an axiom of political economy that labor, assisted by capital exerted upon land, is the primary source of wealth. The three factions of production, then, are land, labor and capital, and the product, if any, is wealth.

Land is defined by political economists with sufficient unanimity to be the earth, and all natural forces and powers incident thereto. This includes the sea and land, rivers and waterfalls, air, light, heat and electricity, the power of fructification, and all other properties of matter which assist in furnishing means to satisfy human desire.

Labor, as applied to production, is defined as human, physical exertion, as modified by, and dependent upon, hereditary traits, mental and moral culture.

Capital is one of the ambiguous terms of political economy. Standard authors define the word as fancy dictates and use it to suit every convenience.

Henry George, in "Progress and Poverty," makes a thorough examination of the nature and relations of capital, in order to give a clear idea of this term. He collates the definitions of numerous authors, shows their inconsistencies and rejecting errors, sets the meets and bounds of the term, so that the idea of what is and is not capital is readily discernable, and then confounds all his subsequent reasoning by falling into the very error he has been combating. To make this plain I quote freely from " Progress and Poverty," chapter ii. He says:

"In general discourse all sorts of things that have a value or will yield a return are vaguely spoken of as capital, while economic writers vary so widely that the term can hardly be said to have a fixed meaning. Let us compare with each other the definitions of a few representative writers:"

"'That part of a man's stock,'" says Adam Smith (book ii., chapter i.), "'which he expects to afford him a revenue is called his capital,' "and the capital of a country or society," he goes on to say, "consists of (1) machines and instruments of trade which facilitate and abridge labor; (2) buildings, not mere dwellings, but which may be considered instruments of trade—such as shops, farm-houses, etc.; (3) improvements of land which better fit it for tillage or culture ; (4) the acquired and useful abilities of all the inhabitants ; (5) money ; (6) provisions in the hands of producers and dealers, from the sale of which they expect to derive a profit; (7) the material of, or partially completed, manufactured articles still in the hands of producers or dealers; (8) completed articles still in the hands of producers or dealers. The first four of these he styles fixed capital and the last four circulating capital, a distinction of which it is not necessary to our purpose to take any note."

Ricardo's definition is :

"Capital is that part of the wealth of a country which

is employed in production, and consists of food, clothing, tools, raw materials, machinery, etc., necessary to give effect to labor."—Principles of Political Economy, chapter v.

"This definition, it will be seen, is very different from that of Adam Smith, as it excludes many of the things which he includes—as acquired talents, articles of mere taste or luxury in the possession of producers or dealers, and includes some things which he excludes—such as food, clothing, etc., in the possession of the consumer."

McCulloch's definition is:

"The capital of a nation really comprises all those portions of the produce of industry existing in it that may be directly employed either to support human existence or to facilitate production."—Notes on Wealth of Nations, book ii., chapter i.

"This definition follows the line of Ricardo's, but is wider. While it excludes everything that is not capable of aiding production it includes everything that is so capable, without reference to actual use or necessity for the use—the horse drawing a pleasure carriage, being, according to McCulloch's view, as he expressly states, as much capital as the horse drawing a plow, because he may, if need arises, be used to draw a plow."

"John Stuart Mill, following the same general line as Ricardo and McCulloch, makes neither the use, nor the capability of use, but the determination to use the test of capital. He says:

"'Whatever things are destined to supply productive labor with the shelter, protection, tools and materials which the work requires, and to feed and otherwise maintain the laborer during the process, are capital.—Principles of Political Economy, book i., chapter iv.

"These quotations sufficiently illustrate the divergence of the masters. Among minor authors the variance is still greater, as a few examples will suffice to show."

"Professor Wayland, whose 'Elements of Political Economy' has long been a favorite text book in American educational institutions, where there has been any pretense of teaching political economy, gives this lucid definition:

"'The word capital is used in two senses. In relation to product it means any substance on which industry is to be exerted. In relation to industry, the material on which industry is about to confer value that on which it has conferred value; the instruments which are used for the conferring of value, as well as the means of sustenance by which the being is supported while he is engaged in performing the operation.'—Elements of Political Economy, book i., chapter i.

"Henry C. Carey, the American apostle of protectionism, defines capital as 'the instrument by which man obtains mastery over nature, including in it the physical and mental powers of man himself.' Professor Perry, a Massachusetts free trader, very properly objects to this, that it hopelessly confuses the boundaries between capital and labor, and then himself hopelessly confuses the boundaries between capital and land by defining capital as 'any valuable thing, outside of man himself, from whose use springs a pecuniary increase or profit.' An English economic writer of high standing, Mr. William Thornton, begins an elaborate examination of the relations of labor and capital ('On Labor') by stating that he will include land with capital, which is very much as if one who proposed to teach algebra should begin with the declaration that he would consider the signs plus and minus as meaning the same thing and having the same value. An American writer, also of high standing, Professor Francis A. Walker, makes the same declaration in his elaborate book on 'The Wages Question.' Another English writer, N. A. Nicholson ('The Science of Exchanges,' London, 1873), seems to cap the climax of absurdity by declaring in one paragraph (p. 26) that 'capital must, of course, be accumulated by saving,' and in the very next paragraph stating that 'the land which produces a crop, the plow which turns the soil, the labor which secures the produce, and the produce itself, if a material profit is to be derived from its employment, are all alike capital.' But how land and labor are to be accumulated by saving them he nowhere condescends to explain. In the same way a standard American writer, Professor Amasa Walker (p. 66, 'Science of Wealth'), first declares that capital arises from the net savings of labor, and then immediately afterward declares that land is capital." * * *

"Now, it makes little difference what name we give to things if, when we use the name, we always keep in view the same things and no others." * * *

"This common sense of the term is that of wealth devoted to procuring more wealth. Dr. Adam Smith correctly expresses this common idea when he says: 'That part of man's stock which he expects to afford him revenue is called his capital.' And the capital of a community is evidently the sum of such individual stocks, or that part of the aggregate stock which is expected to procure more wealth." * * *

"The difficulties which beset the use of the word capital as an exact term, and which are even more strikingly exemplified in current political and social discussions than in the definition of economic writers, arise from two facts: First, that certain classes of things, the possession of which to the individual is precisely equivalent to the possession of capital, are not part of the capital of the community; and second, that things of the same kind may or may not be capital, according to the purpose to which they are devoted.   *   *   *

"Land, labor and capital are the three factors of production. If we remember that capital is thus a term used in contradistinction to land and labor, we at once see that nothing properly included under either one of these terms can be properly classed as capital. * * * A fertile field, a rich vein of ore, a falling stream which supplies power, may give to the possessor advantages equivalent to the possession of capital, but to class such things as capital would be to put an end to the distinction between land and capital, and, so far as they relate to each other, to make the two terms meaningless. * * * In common parlence we often speak of a man's knowledge, skill or industry as constituting his capital; but this is evidently a metaphorical use of language that must be eschewed in reasoning that aims at exactness." *   *   *

"Thus we must exclude from the category of capital, everything that may be included either as land or labor. Doing so, there remain only things which are neither land nor labor, but which have resulted from the union of these two original factors of production. Nothing can be properly capital that does not consist of these—that is to say, nothing can be capital that is not wealth."

" But it is from ambiguities in the use of this inclusive term wealth that many of the ambiguities which beset the term capital are derived."

"As commonly used, the word "wealth" is applied to anything having an exchange value. But when used as a term of political economy it must be limited to a much more definite meaning, because many things are commonly spoken of as wealth which, in taking account of collective or general wealth, cannot be considered as wealth at all. * * * Such are bonds, mortgages, promissory notes, bank bills or other stipulations for the transfer of wealth. * * * Increase in the amount of bonds, mortgages, notes or bank bills cannot increase the wealth of the community that includes as well those who promise to pay as those who are entitled to receive. * * * And all this relative wealth, which, in common thought and speech in legislation and law is undistinguished from actual wealth, could, without the destruction or consumption of anything more than a few drops of ink and a piece of paper, be utterly annihilated." * *

"All things which have an exchange value are, therefore, not wealth, in the only sense in which the term can be used in political economy. Only such things can be wealth, the production of which increases, and the destruction of which decreases the aggregate of wealth." * * *

"Thus, wealth, as alone the term can be used in political economy, consists of natural products that have been secured, moved, combined, separated, or in other ways modified by human exertion, so as to fit them for the gratification of human desires. It is, in other words, labor impressed upon matter in such a way as to store up, as the heat of the sun is stored up in coal, the power of human labor to minister to human desires. Wealth is not the sole object of labor, for labor is also expended in ministering directly to desire; but it is the object and result of what we call productive labor—that is, labor which gives value to material things. Nothing which nature supplies to man, without his labor, is wealth, nor yet does the expenditure of labor result in wealth, unless there is a tangible product which has and retains the power of ministering to desire."

"Now, as capital is wealth devoted to a certain purpose, nothing can be capital which does not fall within this definition of wealth. By recognizing and keeping this in mind, we get rid of misconceptions which vitiate all reasoning in which they are permitted, which befog popular thought, and have led into mazes of contradiction even acute thinkers."

"But though all capital is wealth, all wealth is not capital. Capital is only a part of wealth—that part, namely, which is devoted to the aid of production. It is in drawing this line between the wealth that is and the wealth that is not capital that a second class of misconceptions are likely to occur."   *   *

And, after contrasting the definitions of Mc-Culloch, Ricardo and Mills, and drawing the distinction which must necessarily be made between wealth used for the gratification of desire and capital, he says :

"In all these cases the term capital is used in its commonly understood sense, as that portion of wealth which its owners do not propose to use directly for their own gratification, but for the purpose of obtaining more wealth. In short, by political economists, in everything except their definitions and first principles, as well as by the world at large, 'that part of a man's stock,' to use the words of Adam Smith, 'which he expects to afford him revenue, is called his capital.' This is the only sense in which the term capital expresses any fixed idea —the only sense in which we can, with any clearness, separate it from wealth and contrast it with labor."

It would seem that nothing more need be said to render the term capital easily understood.

The tests of capital, therefore, are:

1st. It must be wealth.

2nd. It must be wealth devoted to production.

The tests of wealth are:

a. It must be a material thing.

b. It must be "secured, combined, separated, or otherwise modified so as to be capable of exchange value, *i. e.*, capable of satisfying human desire;" and

c. A negative test of wealth is: Its destruction must lessen the sum of human wealth.

With what astonishment, if not chagrin, then, do we read Mr. George as he goes on:

"If the articles of actual wealth, existing at a given time in a given community, were presented in situ to a dozen intelligent men who had never read a line of political economy, it is doubtful if they would differ in respect to a single item, as to whether it should be accounted capital or not. 'Money which its owner holds for use in his business or in speculation would be accounted capital;' money set aside for household or personal expenses would not. That part of a farmer's crop held for sale or for seed, or to feed his help in part payment of wages, would be accounted capital; that held for the use of his own family would not be. The horses and carriages of a hackman would be classed as capital, but an equipage kept for the pleasure of its owner would not. So, no one would think of counting as capital the false hair on the head of a woman, the cigar in the mouth of a smoker, or the toy with which a child is playing; but the stock of a hair dealer, of a tobacconist, or the keeper of a toy store would be unhesitatingly set down as capital. A coat which a tailor has made for sale would be accounted as capital, but not the coat he had made for himself. Food in the possession of a hotel keeper, or a restauranter, would be accounted capital, but not the food in the pantry of a housewife, or in the lunch basket of a workman."

Money wealth, indeed! When and where did Mr. George discover that money was wealth? If the reader will turn just ten pages over in " Progress and Poverty" he will find Mr. George declares that one of the "fruitful sources of economic error is the confounding wealth with money;" and here we find him drop into this very common source of economic error as readily as all his predecessors.

For has he not told us, and told us truly, that capital must be wealth. Here he says, money is capital, hence wealth. There he says, and says truly, that it is an economic error to call money wealth.

Mr. George might be forgiven for falling into this "common source" of error, of classing money as wealth, but when he goes further and falls into the exceedingly vulgar error of calling money capital, *i. e.*, "wealth devoted to production," one is lost in astonishment at the ease with which the brightest minds are obscured.

No writer of any eminence, which it has been my privilege to read, anywhere, or in any place, defines money as "devoted to production," under any circumstances. Adam Smith says "that part of a man's stock which he expects to afford him a revenue he calls his capital." Under this he classes money as capital, but he is very careful to point out and emphasize the fact that it is not production. He says, book ii., chapter i.: "Money is neither a material to work upon nor a tool to work with. * * That part of his capital which a dealer is obliged to keep by him unemployed, in ready money, for answering occasional demand, is so much dead stock, which, so long as it remains in this situation, produces nothing either to himself or his country. * * The gold and silver money which circulates in any country and by means of which the produce of its land and labor is annually circulated and distributed to the proper consumer, is, in the same manner as the ready money of the dealer, all 'dead stock.' It is a very valuable part of the capital of the country which produces nothing to the country." And, speaking of the revenues of a country, he furthermore says and demonstrates that money forms no part of the revenues of any country, and although an invaluable part of the stock, or, as he expresses it, the " Great wheel of circulation, the great instrument of commerce, * * is the only part of the circulating capital of a society of which the maintenance can occasion any diminution of their net revenue." Not only not productive, but a positive tax upon the revenues of society.

John Stuart Mill, Science of Political Economy, book i., chapter iv., says: " Capital, by persons wholly unused to reflect on the subject, is supposed to be synonymous with money. To expose this misapprehension would be to repeat what has been said in the introductory chapter. Money is no more synonymous with capital than it is with wealth. Money cannot in itself perform any part of the office of capital, since it can afford no assistance to production."

Nevertheless, the habit of classing money as capital has gone on until everyone seems to think it ought to be classed as such. We meet with it in so called works on political economy, in public prints, we hear it in public discussions, and in the halls of legislation, and in the classroom of our seats of education. Lurking under this seeming harmless garb of a name, are such monstrous errors, such grave and far-reaching consequences, that I am constrained to spare no pains to make the distinctions so plain that no one in future, with any pretentions to scientific culture, need confound capital with money.

The first test is, it must be wealth. Wealth is the product of labor.

Now, all the labor of all the men, from Adam to this day, could not make a dollar, a dime, a penny. They might fashion gold or silver into the form of money, but something else is wanting. Until you have organized society and law, there can be no money.

Money is an invention of society. Its purpose is to represent and exchange value. Now value is an ideal thing. It is not matter, nor a property of matter, nor perceivable by any human sense. No one ever saw, heard or tasted value, or perceived it by the sense of smell or feeling. It is a degree of utility only perceived and estimated by the mind. Money, therefore, has nothing to do with the exchange of material things. This is the province of capital; money carries back and forth their value; here its functions in exchange begin and end.

The Supreme Court of the United States, recognizing this, correctly say: " The gold and silver thing we call a dollar is not the standard of a dollar. It is a representative of it." Money is a material thing, endowed with a legal function to represent a fixed idea of value called a dollar. Without this the coins are no more money than a law book is law, a fire heat, or a magnet magnetism.

To illustrate: A manufacturer of plows starts his factory on Monday morning. Labor uses the machinery and material making plows (wealth). Every day he sells ten plows and is paid the money (distribution). At the end of the week he pays his employes money ; that is, he distributes to each the value of his labor in producing plows, of which the money is a representative. It will at once appear that money is not used in making a plow, painting a plow, handling a plow, shipping a plow, nor anywhere until distribution is made, and then only in passing values, but in no way increasing them.

The third test of wealth made by Mr. George is, "that nothing can be wealth the destruction of which does not decrease the sum of human wealth."

Should we tear up all the paper money, melt

up all the gold and other metal coins, there would remain no money, but the sum of gold, silver and paper, of wealth, is exactly the same. In other words, gold and silver and paper, as money, stand in the same relation as bonds and bills and notes. They are simply the representatives of value.

The laws of increase of capital and money are as varied as their powers and functions. When capital is needed by society, labor proceeds to produce it. When money is needed it cannot be made by labor. Artificial barriers of prejudice, caprice of legislators, and especially the ignorance which pervades all society upon the subject, prevents compliance even with the imperative demands of business.

And lastly, in the return which capital receives for services, and the tax which money receives for its use, we can see the climax of folly of classing money as capital. The return which capital receives is something produced by capital, an addition to existing wealth commonly called profit. The return to money is something taken out of wealth, created by capital and labor, commonly called interest. As to production and distribution, profit is expressed by a plus sign; as to production, the return to money is ex-

pressed by a minus sign　To do, therefore, as
Henry George does, in " Progress and Poverty,"
confound these two distinct things and call them
interest, is to make the sign, — and +, one and
the same thing at the same time, and any reasoning, founded upon an error so palpable, is just as
reasonable as a solution of a problem in algebra,
where no distinction was made as to these signs.
The only use anyone can make of money is to
part with it.　Capital is always actually or con-
structively in possession of the person using it
and procuring its return—money never is.　Any
bookkeeper knows that his interest account for
money borrowed and used by his firm is always
on the opposite side of the ledger to the profit
which accrues from the use of capital.　Money
never increases.　Wherever interest account is
credit, some profit account is debit.

　　Perceiving the one little analogy between
money and capital of "affording revenue," Adam
Smith includes money in his classification of
capital, when, in their origin, their objects, their
functions, their powers, money and capital have
not one thing in common.　To class them as one
is just as logical as to assert : A man has ears, a
horse has ears ; therefore, a man is a horse.　All
writers upon political economy have accepted

this logic. I respectfully dissent, and shall use the term capital to mean : Wealth devoted to production.

This will mean, not simply the making of things, but wealth in all forms and mutations by which it is made fit for consumption and brought to the consumer, and when its consumption is that of increasing or producing more wealth, even then it is capital. That wealth, in process of consumption to satisfy human desire, which might appropriately be called destructive consumption, is not capital. The reward, or return for the use of capital, I shall call profit, as do most writers upon this subject.

That certain invention of society, used for representing and conveying value, I shall call money. Obligations for the payment of money, I shall call money obligations. The return for the privileges of future payments of money, I shall call interest.

The term wages means the payment for human exertion.

The term rent means a part of the return to the owner of land for the use of the original, natural powers of the soil, as will more fully appear when the subject of rent is discussed.

CHAPTER II.

Land, Labor and Capital the Factors of Production.

The contribution which each renders to the increase of wealth.

Land, in Political Economy, stands for the earth and all its powers. Its mines supply all metals and minerals, incipient wealth, from capital to ornament, from engine to ear rings ; coal, stored heat, the source of power unlimited. In the air, burdened with light, heat and moisture, and in her bosom are nurtured all the elements of vegetable life, all powers of adaptation and assimilation, which promote vegetable growth, the ultimate origin of the elements of nutrition, preservation and protection of animal life.

It is the province of labor, with the assistance of capital, to gather from the mines, to smelt, mould and fashion into capital and forms to satisfy desire; to plow and sow, to harvest and garner and grind the grain ; to gather the fleece and flax and cotton; to spin, weave and dye, and finally convey the finished product so as to meet the demand for final distribution.

It is in the province of capital—

1st. To render land more productive by its use as fertilizers, drains, etc., by the growth of trees and vines, and shrubs and the like.

2d. To enable man to use his own powers to greater advantage by employing the spade, plow and machinery upon land.

3d. To multiply the productive power of labor, by utilizing natural forces in driving machinery, such as spindles, looms and planers.

4th. To accomplish what human power could not do by the multiplication of the energy of natural forces through the use of engines and machinery for handling, rolling and forging vast weights of metals, and tackle, for moving and placing large weights required in buildings, bridges and the like.

5th. To vastly facilitate the exchange of products, beyond the ability of animal power, by its employment in railroads and steam navigation.

6th. To store and keep for future consumption by warehouses, graineries, barns and the like.

The introduction of steam power into production, and especially the improvement in exchange, which has been wrought by railroads and steam navigation, has changed in a measure all relations of society, both individual and national. The products of all climes have become interchangeable. Natural possibilities everywhere have been brought within the radius of utility. Where soil and climate render it desirable to pursue different branches of industry, so as to realize the greatest return with least cost, there man can go and be within the sphere of exchange. Where natural powers and resources stand ready to aid labor and capital in farthering production, there can be found supply and demand. All lands become as one land; all lands compete with all other lands; land values become equalized and rent lower. Thus railroad and steam navigation have brought the wheat fields of Minnesota almost as near the markets of Liverpool as those of York or Lancaster, and the grazing grounds of Colorado and Texas as the Highlands of Scotland. In consequence of this, rent has fallen in some parts of England from £5 to 20 shillings. Capital thus changes the entire relation of landlord and tenant.

Although land furnishes all natural opportunities, such opportunities are dependent upon labor for their utility and value. Land is practically worthless without labor. Neither is labor capable of availing itself of the use of land without capital. In the lowest form of existence known to history men had the implements of the chase and the tools of husbandry, and with these the survival of the race was a question for centuries to determine. With the augmented demand, which came with the increase of population, capital became a necessity. Capital is, however, the product of labor. When it is thus shown that the value of land depends upon labor, and the existence and utility of capital is derived from labor, it would seem that labor could always command a just proportion of the joint exertions of the factors of production. That it does not is painfully evident, and that it is a result of unjust social environments I think will be made to appear.

CHAPTER III.

Money as the Factor of Distribution.

Its origin, objects and relation to the factors of production.

If money is not capital, what is it? What are its relations to production?

In the earliest stages of society money is not found. One made the bow and arrow and spear, one caught fish, another followed the chase, all lived in communities, exchanging or holding in common the product of forest and stream. As population increases and society advances, the necessity arises for a more thorough utilization of the productive power of nature. Cultivation, which could easily support one inhabitant to the square mile, must be crowded up to the point of supporting fifty to one hundred to the square mile. Every resource of nature must be pushed to its utmost, every power of man be brought into activity, or society would perish. The division of labor becomes a necessity. One becomes a husbandman, another a mechanic, another a tailor, another a miller. Exchanges become more numerous, complicated and difficult. The farmer, who would have clothing, or boots, or a plow, takes his wheat to the tailor, the shoemaker or the plowmaker, where he finds they do not want wheat, but do want flour; so he goes to the miller, where he finds the water is run low, and so on, through endless exchanges and complications, with consequent loss of time and waste of productive power. Money is an invention of society to prevent just such unnecessary exchanges; to facilitate distribution without exchange of products; to render unnecessary numberless useless, wasteful and costly exchanges. It is an invention which is the outgrowth of the advancement of civilization. It is a necessity to the existence of society. The power to make money inheres in civil government, just as do the powers of preserving peace or of defence in war. Recognizing this, all civil governments determine the character of their coinage, what shall be the material, how assayed, weighed, alloyed, divided; what value each denomination shall represent; how interchangeable, what

devices to prevent counterfeiting; and when so
made as to be readily recognized, they give it
the power of legal tender, which makes it the
legal representative of debts and their value
within the realm.   Money thus constituted becomes the legal unit of estimate of all values and
of the payment of debts, and is distinguished by
this from all other things in society.   The moment wealth is constituted money it ceases to be
governed by any of the laws of wealth, because
it cannot perform any of the functions of wealth
or capital.   It has now gone up higher; has as-
sumed new and important functions.   It is now
a law unto itself.   It has become an agent to
lessen the labor of exchange.

This is the primary use of money, and its consequences are not easily computed and but half
understood.   The most conspicuous are :

1st.   The immense saving of productive power
of labor and capital in expense of exchange to
be invested in further production.

2d.   The possibilities of accomplishing what
is known in political economy as the division of
labor and the consequent increase of work,
which the same number of people are capable of
performing, which Adam Smith, in chapter ii.,
"Wealth of Nations," says, arises " from the in-

creased dexterity in every particular workman ";
"from saving of time lost in passing from one
specie of work to another," and "lastly from the
invention of a great number of machines which
facilitate and abridge labor."

3d. Money renders it possible for labor and
capital, through the great channels of commerce,
to utilize the forces of nature to the best advantage. What I have said as to capital in this respect would be lost were it not for money. This
will become manifest to any one who will take
the trouble to study for himself how it would be
possible to operate a railroad, or manage the
business of a steamship, without money.

In such case, every person desiring freight or
passenger transportation, would be compelled to
bring some product of his labor, which could be
weighed, measured, or subdivided to pay for
passage or transportation. Ordinary products
would be useless to a common carrier. Suppos-
ing it were possible to procure enough gold or
silver to perform the simple exchanges of this
character for the world's carrying trade of to-day,
(which is a very doubtful supposition), even
then every agent would be compelled to assay,
weigh and subdivide these metals, to make
change and payment in each transaction, from a

penny to an eagle, which would so delay and impede transportation, or increase its cost, that seven out of ten railroads now in use would be worthless were money stricken out of existence.

Important as this primary use or function of money is, it has a far greater resultant influence. Every act of paying out money in production, results in storing wealth. Every payment to the laborer, by which his portion of his production is distributed to him, leaves in the hands of him who paid the money the wealth thus created. The result of the distribution which money makes is the storing of wealth, more particularly capital, for future use. This resultant power is in the hands of the possessor of money. He can employ labor and capital to produce wealth, pay wages and profit and have capital. He who has land can borrow money, store capital, and with his labor and capital produce wealth, and afford to pay for the addition to wealth which the capital stored by money produces. He who has money, " dead stock," can demand a portion of the return which the capital stored by the use of his money affords.

Interest, then, is the result of this power of money, to represent and exchange value and store capital. It occurs in the construction of all capital where future returns for use is to repay present advances of value, such as hotels, warehouses, ships, railroads and the like. To labor, which constructs such works, there never can be any payment in kind. Five, ten, or fifty years may elapse before the return will be realized, to pay for the first and last spike driven by labor, and when the return does come there is no tangible product, nothing except valuable services, and these, especially if a year or two in the future, neither stop hunger nor warm the body. Each day the laborer throws up the mound of dirt which will be the thoroughfare of commerce, creating capital of more value than his wages, but he cannot subsist upon this or upon any portion of the production of this capital, present or future. Another, day by day, puts into solid wall his labor, creating capital, a portion of which is his wages. How shall the proportion of this value be given to him to enable him to supply his wants? How is wealth or capital to be stored when there is no product for exchange of kind? It is done by the advance of money. This principle runs through the production of all articles whose consumption in use, continues through a period of time, such as engines, machinery, etc.; also through all articles of consumption, whose completion requires them to go through different hands before ready for distribution. Money pays the labor, *i. e.*, stores the wealth and additional value created by labor in every stage of transition, from raw material to finished product. As a rule, the laborer must subsist upon the result of his labor from week to week, but it rarely occurs that he can use the product of his own labor—as he spins thread or forges steel, he is, in the broadest sense, producing bread. If he needs neither thread nor steel, he does need its equivalent. He gets this by the use of money. Whenever money is used in production, or whenever money is loaned to be used in production, it is to enable labor and capital to store wealth. It is just the reverse process of the ordinary or primitive use of money. That is the subdividing wealth for consumption, this the aggregation of wealth for future use. The following conclusions necessarily result from these premises:

1st. That in some degree all exchanges are limited by the quantity of money in every country.

2nd. That the division of labor, with its momentous results, is practically dependent upon money.

3rd. That money is the means which enables labor and capital to store almost all wealth, and without which the most important and useful capital would not be made or stored.

The rules which may be laid down as embodying the government of these facts and principles in society are as follows:

1st. When money is so scarce as to impede the division of labor, production will necessarily be restricted, as is the case in all half-civilized countries.

2nd. When there is a surplus over and above the necessities of the primary use of money, subject to loan, capital will be stored with this, which, in expectancy, will pay wages, wear and tear (its own reproduction), profit equal to interest, or greater, and interest on the value of product to final distribution.

This is the same as saying that a man will store capital with his own or borrowed money, so long as it will pay and no longer. Now, as money can always be turned into capital, he who has money commands capital; that is to say, he can store capital for any business he may choose. As men naturally select the most profitable business, so they would not loan money at a rate below the amount they could make in the most profitable business open for occupation. Hence, as a rule, money will be used at the highest point of productiveness open to it, in any given condition of society; that is, interest is in accord with the profit made by capital at the highest point of opportunities, which will use the quantity of money in a country.

If there was a given quantity of money in a country, and opportunities sufficient to employ the capital it would store to produce seven per cent., interest would oscillate around seven per cent. If six per cent. then interest would stand at or near six per cent. But money is not, as we have seen, a natural product, nor is it governed by the laws of competition, nor by any other fixed rules. It is a kind of unnatural child of ignorance sired by necessity. There is nowhere any proportion established or any attempt to establish a proportion between its quantity and its functions. One nation regulates it so as to meet the requirements of production at four per cent., others at six, eight or ten.

Now, there never was a country yet which could produce for a population of over ten to the square mile sufficient to pay a net profit of over three per cent. for any length of time upon the

capital necessary in production. Admitting,
then, that the amount of capital stored by money
constitutes but a small portion of the gross capital of the country, it will follow, as a necessity,
that the balance who constitute the great body of
society, must work their capital at a very
low rate, to bring the average down to or below
three per cent. A careful examination of the
actual conditions of society reveals just this, as a
fact, *i. e.*, the largest share of producers, employ
their capital at or near the margin of cultivation,
so, in other words, as to make no profit and just
so as to get average wages. This results from
various causes, even where money under the
rule is allowed to store capital.

Thus, money is dull at six per cent. A man
sees a chance to make profit of six per cent. in a
canning factory. He puts up one. He has not
enough money to store stock and borrows an
equal amount to do this. Hundreds of others
do this, and in other enterprises also. The first
year he does well, makes six per cent., all round
and pays interest. The next year fruit is a little
higher, money a little scarcer, goes up to seven
per cent:, demand a little slack for finished goods.
He foots up and finds his enterprise has made
five per cent. all round, pays seven per cent. on

borrowed money, and it leaves him on his own capital three per cent. The next year he will probably shut down or drag along at about two per cent.

A farmer has land and just one-half the capital which his labor can economically use. He borrows as much money at six per cent. and puts it into crops. Drouth comes, and when he cleans up, he finds, if very lucky, he has three per cent. left upon his capital, all of which goes to pay interest. He worked his own capital for nothing.

But the principal reason, as I stated it above, is because it is not in the wood. The producer does not make profit much above the margin, because there is no such profit to be made. In the United States, where land is subdivided and held under the ordinary laws of competition, take the largest class who occupy the land, the farmers, and they do not on the average make a net increase on the value of land and capital of two per cent. I make this statement deliberately and challenge investigation. In taking a computation there must be taken the price for which land, implements, stock and capital would sell. Enough must be charged to expense to make good all loss in fences, barns, tools, sufficient to

pay taxes, insurance, for all manures and fertilizers to keep land in just equal condition, use of
team, and then must be credited up to wages an
amount equal to the average of mechanic's
wages for every day in the year for each member
of the household who contributes to production
by plowing, seeding, sowing, milking, churning
and the like, and then (well, I will not say anything about the interest on the mortgage, for I
should bring nine farms out of ten in debt), it
will be found I have overstated the net gain of
the farm when I place it at two per cent. When
the thing is sifted to the bottom it shows that
average interest is from two to three times as
great as average profit. All interest is paid out
of profit. If it is not made by the capital stored
by money, then it must be paid out of other
profit, and the interest is ultimately paid by those
who consume the products of the capital stored
by money, and becomes a general tax upon communities. Money takes no chances. Labor and
capital take all chances of production.

Profit and interest, therefore, are not one, are
not equal, do not correspond in quantity, are not
dependent one upon the other; only such profit
as is made at the top of production corresponds
in quantity with interest, or, as was before stated,

at the highest point of production, consistent with the amount of money in circulation. This brings us to the third rule, which is:

If the surplus of money increases, or demand decreases so as to lower interest, land which would not produce net profit equal to interest, will now do so, and be brought into cultivation. Capital will be stored to meet the requirements of manufacturing, mining and transportation enterprises at the lower rate. Should money continue to increase and interest to lower, this would go on until all labor was employed or all resources exhausted.

The reverse would of course be true. As interest advanced, less and less money would be borrowed to store capital, and if it continued no opportunities would exist which would afford a return to pay interest. This third rule is a necessary inference growing out of the second, for what will occur in any particular stage of interest will occur in all.

The views here presented, as to the residuary effect of money, are essentially new, but when examined will be found to be a statement of the common experience of business men everywhere. It illustrated the common way of storing capital.

Telegraphs and railroads are so constructed, mines and manufactories worked and their products stored Within the last forty years, five billions of capital have been thus stored in the United States in making railroads alone, which, under the slow accumulations of a system of barter, would have consumed hundreds of years in their construction, if, indeed, they could ever have been built.

That these plain facts, the result of this effect of money, have not been apprehended by political economists, is due to the confusion of thought consequent upon confounding money with capital by Adam Smith.

As a consequence of this classification he and all of his followers are compelled to call money gold and silver, or gold and silver money, when it is a plain fact that these metals may increase and money decrease, or that money may increase and gold and silver decrease. That the demand for money may increase and demand for gold and silver decrease, or vice versa, or in other words, political economists are put in the dilemma that they have to ride two horses going in opposite directions at one and the same time. This would be considered a very difficult feat anywhere except in political economy, and while

I admit that Adam Smith or John Stuart Mill could accomplish this feat, if any two economists could, yet I think that an analysis of their writings will show how completely they fail, as well as demonstrate every theory advanced by me. This principal is discussed by Adam Smith under the head of "Stock Lent at Interest." He says, book ii., chapter iv.:

" Almost all loans at interest are made in money either of paper or gold or silver. But what the borrower really wants and what the lender really supplies him with is not the money, but the money's worth or the goods which it can purchase. If he wants it as a stock for immediate consumption, it is those goods only which can be placed in that stock. If he wants it as capital for employing industry, it is from those goods only that the industries can be furnished with the tools, materials and maintenance necessary for carrying on their work. By means of the loan the lender, as it were, assigns to the borrower his right to a certain portion of the annual produce of the land and labor of the country to be employed as the borrower pleases. The quantity of stock, therefore, or as it is commonly expressed of money, which can be lent at interest in any country, is not regulated by the value of the money whether paper or coin which serves as the instrument of the different loans made in that country, but by the value of that part of the annual produce, which, as soon as it comes, either from the ground or from the hand of the productive laborers, is destined not only for the replacing a capital, but such a capital as the owner does not care to be at the trouble of employing himself.

As such capitals are commonly lent out and paid back in money, they constitute what is called the monied interest. It is distinct not only from the landed, but from the trading and manufacturing interests, as in the last the owners employ their own capitals. Even in the monied interests, however, the money is, as it were, but the deed of assignment which conveys from one hand to another these capitals which the owners do not care to employ themselves. These capitals may be greater in almost any proportion than the amount of money which serves as the instrument of their conveyance. The same pieces of money successively serving for many different loans as well as for many different purchases. 'A,' for example, lends to 'W' a thousand pounds, with which 'W' immediately purchases of 'B' a thousand pounds' worth of goods. 'B' having no occasion for the money himself lends the identical pieces to 'X,' with which 'X' immediately purchases of 'C' another thousand pounds' worth of goods. 'C' in the same manner and for the same reason lends them to 'Y,' who again purchases with them goods of 'D.' In this manner the same pieces, either of coin or paper, may, in the course of a few days, serve as the instrument of three different loans and three different purchases, each of which is, in value, equal to the whole amount of these pieces. What the three monied men, 'A,' 'B,' 'C,' assign to the three borrowers, 'W,' 'X,' 'Y,' is the power to make those purchases. In this power consists both the value and use of the loan. The stock lent by the three monied men is equal to the value of the goods which can be purchased with it, and it is three times greater than that of the money with which the purchases are made. These loans, however, may all be perfectly well secured, the goods purchased by the different debtors being so employed as in due time to bring back, with a profit, an equal value of coin or paper. And as the same pieces of money can thus serve as the instrument of three different loans to three, or for the same reason, thirty times their value, so they may likewise successfully serve as the instrument of repayment.

"A capital lent at interest may in this manner be considered as an assignment from the lender to the borrower of a certain considerable portion of the annual produce, upon condition that the borrower in return shall, during the continuance of the loan, annually assign to the lender a small portion called the interest; and at the end of it a portion equally considerable with that which has originally been assigned to him, called repayment. Though money, either coin or paper, serves generally as the deed of assignment, both to the smaller and to the more considerable portion, it is itself altogether different from what is assigned by it."

It will be seen that Mr. Smith confines the use of the money to the transfer of things in existence. That he affirms that the object of the loan is not the money, but the capital stored by it. Now, I respectfully ask of Mr. Smith or any of his followers, why of wealth already in existence? Why not future wealth? It is the deed of assignment of labor. It is the deed of assignment of capital. It is the deed of assignment of one using the other. The deed of assignment of all capital, present, past and future. And I am especially grateful to Mr. Smith for showing that

it can be in the hands of one, two or three persons at once. And how in the hands of each it
represents different capital, the condition being
that it shall return a small portion called interest. In other words, Mr. A. can borrow
money, and, instead of buying capital already
made, he can employ hands, pay wages and
profit, and build new machinery. He can put
this to work, build a railroad, open up land, or
do anything which will bring a small net amount
increase to pay back for the loan. This is the
only limitation, and, thanks to Mr. Smith, we
can see how it can go back into the bank, and
in a few days Mr. B. can borrow it, and he can
employ some more labor and produce more
capital; and Mr. D. likewise, and thus inside of
a few months this money as a means constructs
one, two, three engines (that is, distributes value
to the accomplishment of this end), and twenty
men, fifty men, one thousand men, who otherwise would stand idle, would have employment
by the power inherent in money, inherent in
nothing else on the earth, in the earth or under
the earth; the power of authentication and
public credit given by legal tender, the only limit
being labor to use, and opportunities to make the
interest on money.

Turn to Mr. Mill, book iii., chapter xi.: —

"As a specimen of the confused notions entertained respecting the nature of credit we may advert to the exagerated language, so often used respecting its national importance. Credit has a great, but not as many people seem to suppose, a magical power ; it cannot make something out of nothing. How often is an extension of credit talked of as equivalent to a creation of capital, or as if credit actually were capital. It seems strange that there should be any need to point out that credit being only permission to use the capital of another person, the means of production, cannot be increased by it, but only transferred. If the borrower's means of production and of employing labor are increased by the credit given him, the lenders are as much diminished. The same sum cannot be used as capital both by the owner and also by the person to whom it is lent; it cannot supply its entire value in wages, tools and material to two sets of laborers at once. It is true that the capital which A. has borrowed from B., and makes use of it in his business, still forms part of the wealth of B. for other purposes; he can enter into arrangements in reliance on it, and can borrow when needful an equivalent sum on the security of it ; so that to a superficial eye it might seem as if both A. and B. had the use of it at once, but the smallest consideration will show that when B. has parted with his capital the use of it as capital rests with A. alone, and that B. has no other service from it than in so far as his ultimate claim serves him to obtain the use of another capital from a third person, C. All capital not his own, of which any person has really the use, is and must be so much subtracted from the capital of some one else."

This would seem to be the exact contradiction

of the true theory, until we recollect that Mr.
Mill is here talking of one thing and reasoning
about another—is talking about money loaned,
and reasoning about capital. B. did not part
with any capital. He loaned money. A. used
it to procure capital of C., who at once paid labor
and duplicated his capital, and then there were
two capitals where there was but one before.
That is, there is the capital in the hands of A.
and the capital in the hands of C., and the money
in the hands of some other person which represented the same value; in other words, there are
three quantities representing the same amount
as the original money loaned. Mr. Mill tries
here to ride both ways at once. Turn over a
few pages and he tells us that production cannot
be fully exerted without credit, and a little
further on that a man can by the use of credit,
(loaned money), purchase not only as much as
he has money, but as much as he has credit besides. In other words, he can store by the use
of money as much more capital as his real estate
and personal property. That is to say, the inert
matter, land, can be turned into circulating capital to aid labor in production by the use of
money.

This is the gist of the whole matter. Money

is the evidence of public credit,—public credit
mobilized, by which all the slow accumulation
of ages can be turned into circulating—creative
capital. This public credit is not wealth (gold
and silver cease to be wealth when made money),
but the evidence that there is behind the coin or
paper, sufficient of public power and wealth to
make it good to the holder, and that whatever it
by law represents, is to be had for it in exchange
at any time, and such being its power and function, it represents not only the power to gather
past labor in the form of wealth, as Mr. Mill and
Mr. Smith assert, but it represents the power to
gather all future capacities of land and labor, the
only limit being the capacity of labor, and opportunities to pay interest exacted by money in
proportion to use. Mr. Mill, Smith and all
other writers down to Bastiat and George, miss
all this, because, as just quoted, they have money
mixed up with capital, and it is impossible to
recognize money as a distributor, while it is
classed as a producer, and although every decade
has afforded disproof of one or another of the
current theories growing out of this classification,
although every generation has shown that they
are not based upon any principle or governed
by any system, as evinced by the blind groping

of different governments in monetary matters, such as demonetizing and remonetizing metals, changing coinage laws, making paper money, suspension of payments—during which more than one government would have gone to the wall, had they not in practice disregarded such teachings—yet, economic writers have not made one step forward to meet the wants of society. They have reiterated these sophisms until the public mind is befogged; until men do not know whether they have or have not any interest in money matters, whether they ought or ought not to interest themselves in this behalf, when, in fact, the power of money permeates all production, affects the welfare and happiness of every member of society, the bread in every man's mouth, is the bearer of one of the highest functions of government; a function higher than capital, for it commands capital; higher than labor, for it commands labor; higher than wealth, for it commands wealth, dictates war and peace, and determines the issues of civilization.

CHAPTER IV.

Of various theories heretofore advanced to account for existing conditions and their insufficiency.

Theories without number have been advanced in explanation of the conditions which we are investigating. That poverty and distress are to be found amidst illimitable power of production, and a constantly increasing surplus product, is an enigma which forces itself upon the dullest comprehension. We accordingly find it the theme of debates in clubs, the burden of vapid discussions of a quasi-scientific nature, cropping out in the halls of legislation, in assumptious maudlings of the public press, until everyone, high or low, are ready with a solution of the problem, while all the time, the lean finger of want points to her children, as an emphatic denial that any sufficient explanation has ever been given of these anomilies in the social organism.

Of all theories advanced, which claim attention on scientific grounds, no one has attained such prominence or maintained such undisputed sway as that to which Malthus has given his name. Observing that during a given period of time population was increased in a greater ratio than subsistence, Malthus adduced and promulgated it as a general law that the pressure of population against subsistence is the necessary and inevitable cause of poverty among men. That is to say, that a constantly increasing population, with a relative diminution of production, would drive the great mass of humanity to the verge of maintenance, and ultimately to the lowest point at which human being can live and reproduce.

Strange as it may now seem, this doctrine, supported by its apparent mathematical genesis, became a settled dictum of political ethics. Tactily, if not wholly, approved by all leading political economists, complacently commented on by such writers as Ricardo and Mill, it was never seriously challenged until the appearance of " Progress and Poverty."

Mr. George, in discussing this theory, shows that there is no general law by which population is increased; that population advances and recedes; that the increase of population tends to increase productive power, and that as subsistance is but one part of production, the increase of population would tend to a better state of living were there no mal-adjustments of society.

He also discusses the argument in favor of this theory, drawn by analogy from the multifarious increase of animals and plants, and shows that the argument really proves the reverse of the theory, as this wonderful fecundity under the intelligent direction of man can always be made an increasing source of support.

And finally, by facts, he shows that the marvelous increase of productive power, through and by means of invention to use the occult forces of nature, render it certain that whatever might have been the cause at any time in history, at the present time this law has no potency whatever. And I might add that a report of a bureau of the government, lately made, shows that a population of fifty millions of people can produce supplies for a population of one hundred millions, so whatever may be the cause of poverty it is not the want of the abundant supplies of the necessities of life.

Having thus disposed of Malthus, Mr. George gives his own theory. He says "the reason why

wages tend to a minimum which will give but a
bare living" is because of rent; *i. e.*, the rise of
land values, and this is occasioned by the private
ownership of land; that as population increases
men are driven to poorer land, relatively; that
by the law of rent, wages are determined by the
margin of cultivation, *i. e.*, the poorest land in
use.   All that is received on land by the cultivation at the margin is wages and profit.   All that
is received on better land above this is rent.   And
he concludes that rent absorbs all production except wages and profit at the margin.   As the
margin goes down wages fall until labor gets no
more than a bare living.   His proposed remedy
is to destroy all private ownership in land by a
tax equal to its rental value, which shall go to
the State in lieu of all other taxes.

As his work "Progress and Poverty" has many
readers and his theory many adherents, and as I
deem it fully as misleading as the doctrines of
Malthus, I shall examine its claims for consideration carefully before I proceed.

The theory of Mr. George is based upon the
law of rent, as promulgated and explained by
Ricardo, and it is little else than these doctrines,
enlarged and extended, on an assumption that

they can be made applicable to the whole of society.

Mr. Ricardo says, in "Principles of Economy," chapter ii., that "Rent is that portion of the produce of the earth, which is paid to the landlord for the use of the original and indestructable powers of the soil. * *

"In a new country when there is an abundance of fertile land compared with the population, and when, therefore, it is only necessary to cultivate No. 1, the whole production will belong to the cultivator and will be the profits of the stock which he advances. * *

"When, in the progress of society, land of a second degree of fertility is taken into cultivation, rent immediately commences upon the first quality, and the amount of rent will depend upon the difference of these two portions of land."

Thus, Ricardo confines rent to the difference between the highest and lowest production, and credits all produced on the poorest land to profit and wages. He strictly confines the law "to the use of the original and indestructable powers of the soil." He carefully excludes all improvements or additions to land, all mines, quarries and timber, and states distinctly that payment for the use of improvements or for the privilege of removing coal or timber is not paid for rent.

Mr. George endorses these rules in the main, and with Ricardo, affirms:

1st. That all the product at the margin is wages and profit. (He calls it interest.)

2d. That all received from better land is rent, wages and profit.

But he affirms:

3d. That Ricardo did not fully understand the law himself, and later dictum holds that the law is broad enough to include all industries, and does govern wages everywhere.

In these two first propositions Mr. George falls headlong into the pit he dug for himself when he confounded money with capital. Having classed money as capital, he is bound to class interest as profit, and this necessitates his dividing all production just as he does, because as he has no factors of production but land, labor and capital, and no factor of distribution at all, he, from his standpoint, logically concludes that all the production must go to one of these factors; that is, all production must go to land, labor and capital, or is divided to land as rent, to capital as profit (or interest), to labor as wages; just in accordance with the above statement of Ricardo. This runs him up against a circumstance. In book ii , chapter iv., he discusses under the head of "Spurious Capital" such things as bonds, notes, mortgages and the like, which he very properly states are not capital, only representatives of capital. Nevertheless, he knows that there is distributed annually to the holders of this "Spurious Capital" a large amount of that same production. Now, where does he account for this payment in his distribution? He cannot say it goes to capital, for bonds or notes are not capital; not to labor or rent, certainly. He has not done anything with it at all. He has no place to put it under his classification. This payment to "Spurious Capital" comes out of production, but cannot be paid to any factor of production mentioned in Ricardo's law. The law is not a full statement of distribution. It must have another factor, the factor of distribution, i e., money. Then there is a place found to distribute this payment to "Spurious Capital." It is interest, and the statement can then be properly made of production. It is:

Production $=$ Rent $+$ wages $+$ profit $+$ interest. Or,

Production $-$ Interest $=$ rent, wages and profit.

In other words, Mr. George proceeds to make distribution without any reference to the payment of these vast sums of money, as interest, upon this character of obligations and in utter oblivion of the effect upon results. None of them are capital, and the money was not paid on account of capital, or to capital, or to any one for the use of capital. They are national, state, municipal, town, county and corporate bonds. All railroad, turnpike, water or sewer bonds, mortgages, promissory notes, discounts of all private, state or national banks, etc., etc. In brief, the total of such payments, each year, in the United States alone, amounts to the sum of $1,200,000,-000, and I presume they are no less, proportionately, in other countries; a sum too great for comprehension, but, to give some idea, we will suppose all voters are laborers, and that in round numbers they are $10,000,000, and that this sum paid to "Spurious Capital" would represent the labor of the whole body of such voters at $1.50 per day for seventy-five days each year, or just about one-quarter of the gross earnings of labor. All this is, by this rule of Ricardo and mode of distribution, accredited to rent, wages and profit, when it actually goes to some one else. The interest paid to these bonds comes out of production, but it is not paid to capital or land or labor. It is paid to the gentlemen who furnish the agent of distribution, called money, as payment for its services, and in that capacity and no other.

This solution of Mr. George is very much as though he should attempt to solve a problem in algebra as follows, to wit:

Three known streams (R. W. and P.) run into a cask; the spigot (I.) is wide open all the time; how much in the cask, without taking any account of the spigot? He fails. There is no solution. Omnipotence could not do it.

The law of Ricardo is not broad enough to cover the field of production. It leaves out one of the factors everywhere present, which is actively modifying the effect of the law. It forgets the spigot. Even if it is good, so far as it goes, where then does it go? We cannot say it governs the margin or wages, or even rent, until we know what modifying influences are exerted by this other factor which it ignores.

I have shown that capital changes the margin, raises and lowers rent, now money controls the storing of capital. If, then, the margin controls wages, and capital controls the margin, and money controls capital, which controls?

I think that, taking into account these modifying influences in open competition in production, the law of Ricardo has more of a fanciful than a real influence in society. Wrong thus in fundamental principles it must contradict obvious facts.

Rent potential is not rent actual. The power to demand rent does not compel any one to produce rent, nor does it determine who receives the rent, as a simple illustration will show: "A." works land which produces 3 per cent., with borrowed capital at 6 per cent., of one-half the value of the land. Borrowed capital gets the whole product.

"B." owns land. He puts a mortgage upon it of one-third its value at 6 per cent. Who gets one-half the rent?

If the theory of Mr. George was true, all anyone would be compelled to do would be to borrow money, buy land and let rent make him rich. He might succeed once in a thousand times, but it would hardly do for the whole community to engage such a belief. The universal truth known to all business men, that land is held as security for loans of money at not to exceed one-half its value, and then only for a limited time, is evidence that there is something which absorbs production faster than land values.

One of the writers upon land values, I think it

is Cary, by a careful computation of the amount of capital and labor expended upon land, demonstrates that the cost of capital, adding average interest upon money, together with the cost of labor at margin, wages, and, like interest, would exceed the total value of land and improvements. And why should not capital have its compensation and labor its reward?

What is reckoned as land values, is not natural power, but the power given to it by adding labor and capital, and when unoccupied land rises in value, it is the result of the contributions of all the owners alike, and where land is left free to the ordinary rules of competition is the most universal, and as each one in the community have contributed to this advance, is the most equitable distribution of advancing wealth.

That labor and capital are supreme, and not controlled by the margin, is proven by the fact that, whenever land is left open to competition, labor will own the land. Where landed aristocracies exist, it has been found necessary, in order to keep the land from following the natural law of acquisition, to interpose legal barriers, such as laws of entail. This has lately been illustrated, in the attitude of the Gladstone ministry toward the Irish people. They proposed to subject the land of Ireland, enhanced in value by hundreds of years of cultivation, to a term of purchase of thirty years, with money at low rate, and the Irish nation, which has been kept from the land by the operation of monopolistic laws, hail this as a means of giving the land to the people.

The fact is that labor employed directly upon land in the production of raw products, giving it rent and profit and all as wages, works the hardest, the most hours, and for the poorest compensation of any portion of the community. No millionaires are found among them, and though, by a lucky purchase of land, in the midst of a growing and prosperous community, many may be made wealthy, and one Astor, a many times millionaire, thousands upon thousands find themselves land poor, while millionaires multiply by thousands, none of whose acquisitions can be traced to the Ricardo law of rent.

The disproof of the theory of Henry George, is found by taking his sylogism in reversion. If the cause of poverty is rent, no poverty can exist where opportunities are free above the margin. This condition exists now, did yesterday and has always existed in the United States. Yet there are those who don't work, can't get work, and would be glad to work at one-half the wages made upon the poorest land in use to-day. Why don't they work? Let the poorest, half-starved, half-fed laborer, just walk either way half across the island of New York, and in front of him is land plenty and free. There is the East River and the North River, and the boundless ocean just beyond—land, land all. Take, use, occupy without stint and without price. It is above the margin, for thousands are using it every moment. Why don't any believer in Mr. George do it? He tells them that the reason wages are so good in new countries, is because a man can step over on the next quarter section and work for himself. Any man can make a boat as cheap as he can make a house. Any man can own a fair canal boat as cheap as he can buy a team, a plow, seed, planters, and break the soil and open up a prairie farm. Why don't they occupy? Why, within six days' walk of New York city are farms which could always be had for taxes—can be occupied for twenty years without rent. Why don't the poor, starving humanity walk out and enjoy a feast of fat things in this new-found way of becoming well fed?

The theory of Mr. George is not one that touches the wants of those who need help. All he proposes is a little better divide of the present production, making these who are in, a little more comfortable. Those who are out, who are below the margin, who don't work, or but half the time, they want no divide of rent. If all divided, it would not amount to a day's work a year. What they want is three hundred days' work each year. They want the wonderful resources everywhere present, around and above them, opened up and made available to them, so with songs of joy they can go out and gather with their labor, and bind and bring in the golden sheaves of plenty, to homes where gladness and contentment reign.

The pretty pictures which Mr. George draws of times when nobody shall pay taxes, except those who occupy lands, throws into relief another, which, under existing laws, but more especially under the arrangements proposed by Mr. George, might be drawn.

Down in the valley, the capitalist places his mill, (capital) upon a barren rock, worth nothing. In this he collects machinery of the value of hundreds of thousands of dollars. Around go the wheels merrily, driven by an engine (capital), fired by coal, and scatters his products to the four winds, collecting profits by thousands, and pays wages at the maximum because he pays no rent or taxes. One of his employees looks longingly upon a little glebe on the hillside, in full view, and, collecting the remnant of his wages, he occupies the same under Mr. George's rent-tax arrangement.

He plows a little land, not much, for every furrow adds to the value of the land and rent. He plants a few trees, for, as they grow, the tax gatherer will surely increase the rent (Mr. George says everything which becomes indissolubly attached to the soil is land), and so he toils from sun to sun, and his crops grow, and his rent grows. By and by comes a June frost and the rent is not paid, and the tax gatherer exposes his little stock to sale. No one bids among his neighbors, for they are in as much trouble as he. Up steps the mill owner, and out of the profits which pay no taxes or rent, buys his improvements, and then sells them to him or loans them to him at such rate of interest as to make him his slave, worse than the man at the margin.

Who can prevent it? What can prevent it? Mr. George don't answer.

I shall try to do so.

BOOK II.

DISTRIBUTION.

In what manner the products of industry, are appropriated, or shared by different classes in society.

INTRODUCTION.

Four classes divide the products of labor—to land goes rent, to labor wages, to capital profit and to money interest. Laws of distribution not understood and why.

From what has already been written, I think it will readily be admitted, that the factors of production are not responsible for the unequal conditions of society, and that no one of them is a necessary bar to the equal enjoyment of the fruits of industry. I shall, therefore, turn to the law of distribution, in the hope of finding the process by which a few gather the bulk of the products of labor, a large majority are reduced to a bare living and many to absolute want. The obvious injustice of the results of prevailing laws of distribution have led to the promulgation of many theories intended to mitigate the evil consequences flowing therefrom. These may be classified generally as belonging to one or the other of opposite theories of government: On the one hand socialism, or that class who claim that it is the function of government to take charge and control production and distribution for the equal benefit of all; on the other hand, the government of freedom, where the duties of government interfere with individual action, only enough to enforce the possibility of equal competition. This latter theory of free competition, is the one upon which is built advanced civilization, and is generally conceded to be the true theory of government. Present results of distribution cast doubt upon this claim, and unless it can be shown that the laws of distribution are controlled by social or political enactments, which contravene their just action under free competition, the claims of socialism are well nigh established. I think it can be shown that they are thus controlled, and that the power vests in government, which, properly executed, will result in their operation in conformity to the requirements of justice, equality and perfect freedom.

The process or manner of production and distribution, stated in brief, is as follows:

Labor, using capital upon land, produces raw products. Capital and labor transport and deliver raw product to the merchant, who distributes back the value of the same to land, labor and capital, by the payment of money. The merchant ships them to the manufacturer and receives the amount of the original purchase, adding thereto, storage, interest, wages and transportation. Labor uses capital in the form of machinery; grinds, spins, weaves and fashions raw products for consumption, and delivers the finished product to middle men, who again distribute to the manufacturer the original value, the added value, while in the merchants the transporters and the manufacturers' hands. The middle men deliver these finished products for final consumption, when all men get the real pay for labor, for profit and for rent. Mr. Adam Smith says: "The real wages of labor are the products of labor."

To illustrate: Labor, using the horse and plow, prepares the land, plants cotton seed, tends the plants, picks the cotton; with machinery gins, bales, and transports raw cotton to the merchant or broker, who exchanges money for the same, by which is distributed to each factor of production its share of the product; to land rent, to labor wages, to capital profit. And now the price of the cotton stands as, (rent + wages + profit). The broker stores it and ships it to the manufacturer. He adds to the original price, interest on money, wages for handling; also his own wages, storage (rent and profit); also the cost of transportation, and this when analyzed is, rent + wages+profit+interest. The cost of the cotton now stands: $(R.+W.+P.)+(R.+W.+P.+I.)+(R.+W.+P.+I.)$, the value of all of which have been distributed to each of the several factors by money. And so on, through each successive stage of spinning, weaving, transporting, until, in finished cloth, are concentrated all the innumerable items of wages, rent, profit and interest. This men receive and pay back the money which they had received as the representative of wages, profit, interest or rent, and thus have the real object of all human effort, that which satisfies human desires. That which is received as wages is always composed of $R.+W.+P.+I.$

The process of production and distribution, from their incipiency to finality, go on incessantly in society. Distribution is the indispensible link in the chain of production, and both together constitute the warp and woof of the endless web we call agriculture, manufacture and commerce. All the products of industry are intended for consumption, that is, to satisfy human desire. Money, in an economic sense, is never consumed and satisfies no want of man; and, while it appears between every stage of production, it adds nothing to the product or its value. It is always an exchange of equivalents—always as a distributor, never as a producer. While it adds nothing to value it almost always adds to cost. While, therefore, it is proper to say that the factors of production are three, land, labor and capital; when we come to distribution, there are four factors which divide the product.

Land, labor and capital produce.

Land, labor, capital and money divide the product.

Or, as we have designated, the proportion heretofore which goes to land as rent, to labor as wages, to capital as profit, and to money as interest, the proper algebraic expression would be: Production$=R.+W.+P.+I.$

In order to arrive at any just appreciation of the
laws of distribution, it will be necessary to ascertain the relation of each factor of distribution,
also the amount of the gross product, which is
naturally due and appropriated by each. It will
not only be necessary to apprehend these laws,
but their relation, and effect upon each other, for
they are evidently correlative. What goes to
wages and why, cannot be ascertained until we
know what goes to rent, profit and interest, and
why. In a given state of production wages cannot rise, unless one or all the other factors of
distribution fall. And what is the most extraordinary part of the whole matter is, that I am
compelled to discover and bring to light all the
laws of distribution, as well as their relation and
co-ordination. All political economists have
failed to apprehend these laws or their relations.
They each have theories of their own, and all
seemingly start in from the same premises, go
by different roads to different conclusions, one,
apparently, as plausible as the others. What is
so seemingly strange is not at all strange, after
a little examination. We have not very far to
go to find the cause. It has its origin in the
fruitful source of ambiguity we have been point-
ing out from the beginning. It is the failure of

these economists to see the logic of their own work. Smith, Mill, Ricardo, Bastiat, in fact all economic writers, both great and small, assert that money is a distributor of wealth, not a producer. They call the return to money interest, as Adam Smith says, " A derivitive revenue." They call the return to capital, profit, yet, when they come to distribute wealth, they never make any place for interest. As Mill says, the whole community for the purpose of distribution, consists of three classes, landlords, laborers and capitalists, and they proceed to try to show how all wealth produced is divided between them. Now, any child can see, as do all these economists, that the holder of interest-bearing notes at six per cent., of the amount of one hundred thousand dollars, is drawing each year, as interest, six thousand dollars of wealth out of production. It is not the product of the notes, or of the money, not paid to capital, or the owner of capital, because the notes are not capital. How can you make any sensible division between rent, wages and profit until you have ascertained the amount of interest and taken it out? It cannot be done. Interest modifies the amount which can go to the other factors of production, under all circumstances, to the extent of its gross amount. It again modifies their proportion as it rises and as it falls, and, as I have shown, it modifies the power of labor to produce capital, to increase capital; it modifies the employment of labor, the quantity of production, changes profit, absorbs rent, and yet it is entirely left out of every work on political economy as a part of distribution.

Startling as it may seem, I am justified in saying that there has never been any exposition of the laws of distribution worthy of any consideration whatever, or that have approximated to the explanation of existing facts. They are a cut and a try to fit impossible theories to exact facts.

Hence, it is not surprising to find Mr. Adam Smith telling us, that the laboring classes in England have steadily improved in the last two centuries, and Malthus, a few years later, telling us that the pressure of population was steadily driving men to the verge of poverty; and to find Ricardo asserting that wages must go up, and Mr. George that they must go steadily down, both basing their theories upon the same supposed law. I shall, therefore, be compelled, at this late day, to go before and open up the road to unjust and just distribution.

The compensation to the loaners of money,

being a derivitive revenue, comes out of the factors of production, *i. e.*, reduces the amount
which goes to one or all of them. It must come
out before distribution to R., W. and P. As production stands ready for distribution, it should
be expressed therefore:

Production—I.$=$R.$+$W.$+$P.

Now, under existing conditions, and those
which have existed, when the law of competition
is supposed to have its sway, every laborer is a
competitor with every other laborer. Along
this class, if nowhere else, does the law of
competition hold perpetual sway, so that whatever has been the amount of production to be
distributed, it has always been naturally, or by
social adjustment, arranged so that this competition was kept keen and constant; enough to drive
the laborer to about the lowest point of subsistence possible to maintain existence. From which
circumstance all economists, without really knowing the cause, claim that this is the natural condition of wages, and have framed their theories
accordingly.

This sum, that is the total of wages, must
come out of production at all events, or the destruction of society will ensue.

It is safe, in an approximate estimate, to say,

that this is consumed each year, and that the remainder is all that can be divided between rent, profit and interest. This is the net income of society, or the average increase of wealth. Now, as I have shown, interest is a "derivitive revenue:" a sum certain—takes no chances—and must come out before profit or rent. If, therefore, interest equals this net revenue there will be nothing left for profit and rent. Profit and rent are the uncertain factors.

If there is a surplus, after paying interest, it will go to profit and rent, and if they do not get all, wages may rise. These propositions may be stated succinctly thus:

Production—consumption=net revenue.

Net revenue may be less than interest, in which case the balance of community go farther in debt to the venders of money.

Net revenue may be about equal to interest, when society will just pay expenses, and venders of money will receive all surplus production

Net revenue may be more than interest, when interest will be paid, something go to profit and rent, and possibly to wages.

Every one of these conditions are possible in any nation, have occurred in almost all, and in them is the explanation of relations, which can be understood under no system of political economy extant. They are the arbiters of destiny. The tread of their feet is the march of centuries, and as they pass and repass the song of joy or the wail of anguish has come up through the ages.

CHAPTER I.

RENT AND THE LAW OF RENT.

Rent is the compensation for the original and
    indestructible powers of land—Is limited to
    the insignificant difference of the natural
    productiveness of the soil.

The extent to which rent enters into distribution, and the relation it bears to the other factors of distribution, is modified by two considerations :

1st.   The extent of the field of production
over which rent extends.

2nd.   The amount of the production which
rent absorbs where it prevails.

It is self-evident that the influence of rent
upon the other factors of distribution, will be felt
only in a modified sense in any field of production, where rent does not directly enter.   Thus,

the seas and oceans are always open to labor and capital, and subject to interest. They are free to any and everyone. If, then, upon all other fields of production, it were true that wages were driven low by rent, here would be a resort for labor which would modify the effect of wages upon land. The seas and oceans, lakes and navigable rivers, must be excluded when we seek to define the law of rent, or its influence upon wages. Here wages are all the products over profit and interest. The same may be said of all professions, bankers, musicians, teachers, public officers and soldiers. Rent neither enters into, absorbs, or modifies their wages, except incidentally.

In the second place, from all calculations upon rent must be excluded all improvements upon land, and all values commonly accredited to land from such improvements. Ricardo says, "Principles of Political Economy," chapter ii.:

"Rent is that portion of the produce of the earth which is paid to the landlord for the use of the original and indestructible powers of the soil. It is often, however, confounded with the interest and profit of capital, and, in popular language, the term is applied to whatever is annually paid by a farmer to his landlord. If, of two adjoining farms of the same extent and of the same

natural fertility, one had all the conveniences of farming
buildings, and, besides, were properly drained and
manured, and advantageously divided by hedges, fences
and walls, while the other had none of these advantages,
more remuneration would be naturally paid for the use
of one than for the use of the other; yet, in both cases,
this remuneration would be called rent. But it is evident that a portion only of the money annually to be
paid for the improved farm would be given for the original and indestructible powers of the soil. The other
portion would be paid for the use of capital which had
been employed in ameliorating the quality of the land,
and in erecting such buildings as were necessary to secure and preserve the product. Adam Smith sometimes
speaks of rent in the strict sense to which I am desirous
of confining it, but more often in the popular sense in
which the term is usually employed. He tells us that
the demand for timber, and its consequent high price in
the more southern counties of Europe, caused a rent to
be paid for forests in Norway which could before afford
no rent. Is it not, however, evident that the person who
paid what he thus calls rent paid it in consideration of a
valuable commodity which was then standing on the
land, and that he actually repaid himself with a profit by
the sale of the timber? If, indeed, after the timber was
removed, and compensation were paid to the landlord for
the use of the land for the purpose of growing timber, or
any other product, with a view of future demand, such
compensation might justly be called rent, because it
would be paid for the productive powers of the land; but
in the case stated by Adam Smith, the compensation was
paid for the liberty of removing and selling the timber,
and not for the liberty of growing it. He speaks also of
the rent of coal mines and of stone quarries, to which

the same observation is applicable, that the compensation given for the mine or quarry, is paid for the value of the coal or stone, which can be removed from them, and has no connection with the original and indestructible powers of the land.

"This is a distinction of great importance, in any inquiry concerning rent and profit, for it is found that the laws which regulate the progress of rent are widely different from those which regulate the progress of profit and seldom operate in the same direction."

Thus, if Mr. Ricardo knew anything of the law which bears his name, before we commence to compute what rent absorbs, we must exclude all value added by fences, ditches, tile, all additions of fertility by plow, all trees planted, all vines and shrubs, houses, out-houses and barns and graneries. Whatever portion of the product upon agricultural land, which is necessary to be used to store, to keep and maintain these improvements is paid to labor and capital, and is the absortion of wages and profit, and not of rent. The improvements upon agricultural land amount, probably, to three-tenths of its assessed value, and one-tenth of its real value. Also, we must exclude all the valuation of all mines of coal or iron, all quarries, all standing timber, and remember that all labor employed in removing and marketing these products is not governed by rent, or the law of rent.

In the third place, the value of land which arises from other causes than its natural powers of productiveness, or the relative worth by reason of its nearness to market, must be totally excluded in calculated rent or its influence upon wages. Thus, the price of all land used exclusively as a place upon which to erect and use capital is governed by the law of profit, not that of rent. A city lot upon which is placed a manufacturing establishment may be valued at thousands of dollars, but it owes its value to the productiveness of capital planted thereon, and not to the original and indestructible powers of land. All the original powers used under such circumstances, are the powers of attraction of gravitation to hold the building down, and the power of inertia to hold the building up. Rent is the return for the contribution which the powers of land afford to production—a part of this contribution. Where there is no such contribution there can be no rent. The rental value of a city lot is what it would be worth to cultivate. The increased price arises not from increased production or price of production, but from the increased power of capital and money to absorb production—to absorb production in excess of cost of labor and replacement of capital; in other words, to get profit and interest. It is on precisely the same principle as an investment at interest and on the same grounds; be cause the capital stored upon it will pay wages, interest upon the value of the land, and profit equal to interest, on the capital employed. If there was no interest or profit there could be no increased value in the land. This increased value or price of land is erroneously called the "unearned increment" in land, because it arises from the increased exchange by reason of the increase of population. It is really the "unearned increment" of the power of capital and money to absorb production, and has no relation to rent whatever. Mr. Ricardo always made this clear. Mr. George and many others are confused by not making a distinction so palpable. So, all the price which attaches to land in a manufacturing town and large cities, or in their vicinity, which are valued very high because of their desirableness for location for homes, on account of nearness to schools, lyceums and social intercourse; it is not on any principle of productiveness, nor is it the representative of economic rent, past, present or potential, but that of the means of satisfying taste and desire, and it would be just as correct to call a pleasure carriage capital, as to call such price land values, in the sense of rent values.

In the fourth place, in calculating the relative power of rent to absorb the products of industry, we must exclude all factories, workshops, mills in which all the products are almost exclusively composed of $P.+W.+I.$ and rent hardly enters; also all railroads and telegraphs, as these employ, of capital to land (mostly easements in land), in about the proportion of twenty to one, and rent can absorb but this proportionate trifle to decrease wages.

After we have thus excluded from the influence of rent the great bulk of the field of production, and brought it down, as, in fact, it really should be, and always is by Ricardo, to the natural powers to produce, as they stood before the hand of man had wrought any change; in the fifth place, it must be remembered that rent is not all the return which is given by these natural powers, but the difference between the highest and lowest production, after paying interest, wages and profit, of land necessarily used for agricultural purposes. Thus, if at the margin, land which is equal to the poorest land in use, on the average, is held at $15 per acre; for in stance, in Dakota or Kansas and land in the

state of New York, which was never marked
(but away from the speculative influence noted
above and which has produced what might be
termed fancy prices), should be found to be
worth $40 per acre, the difference, or $25 per
acre, would be the rental value of the best land,
according to Ricardo, and the rent would be the
average net increase of wealth upon land, or
about 2 per cent., or about 50 cents, per annum
per acre. On such statement this would be the
total of the production which could be credited
to economic rent, and I think the statement is
not far from correct. [Table iii. of the appendix
shows that the actual return in the United States
for 1880 was 25 cents per acre for all agricultural land, assuming the farmer paid no interest.
This would make, say 50 cents for the highest
rent and from that down to zero. How much of
this is creditable to speculative value, or is required to make good the profit on capital, which
has as good a right to the same as the land, it is
impossible to guess.]

While this as a general statement, is correct,
yet it must always be borne in mind that it matters not what the price, or difference in price of
land, if the land at the margin produces enough
more corn or other products, so that when mar-

keted the net receipts are equal, there is as between these lands no economic rent. That is to
say, if a farmer in Kansas produced sixty bushels
of corn to the acre, which nets him at the crib
20 cents per bushel, and the New York farmer
on the same expenditure of capital and labor
produces forty bushels, which nets him 30 cents,
as between these lands there is no economic
rent; no matter what their price, and so of cotton and wool. Cheap transportation and change
of markets constantly equalize the relative productiveness of land, and should the time come,
that freights should be reduced to a minimum,
the high priced lands of the East would cease to
receive rent at all, and the lands still lower in
price would receive rent, its relative natural productiveness overbalancing the nearness of the
other to market. And so of cotton or wool,
lands which cost nothing comparatively being
far from markets and not desirable for heavy
cereals, producing products, whose cost of transportation is relatively very low, as compared
with their price, such lands may bring a large
return to the acre and have economic rent.

When the arbitrary power of rent is thus reduced almost to zero, it must again be curtailed

in an amount which will, as far as possible, equalize the profits of capital.

It is a proposition that will not be disputed that capital used upon land increases far below the rate of capital expended upon the products of land. Land is productiveless without capital and labor, and capital will not seek land only, as I have shown, with the hope of return equal to the average return from capital, or from necessity. Therefore, when capital is used voluntarily upon land it must and does demand its return before rent. If there is not enough return to pay capital and rent, capital will have its return or will be turned into other channels. In either event rent suffers.

I have thus brought the influence of rent upon the other factors of production to the place it occupies in distribution, by the law of Ricardo. The amount of its influence is so insignificant as to be hardly perceptible under any system where land is free to purchase and sale; but the story does not end here; this is not the end of distribution. When the farmer has gathered his products into his graneries, which constitutes his rent, wages and profit, or the land owner his proportion in money or kind, which constitutes his rent, then with him commences distribution.

He must then exchange these things for those things which go to supply necessities, such as clothing, groceries, doctors' bills, education, luxuries, fuel. Let us see how he stands at the end of distribution, and what has become of his rent and wages. In speaking of the products which comes from land, and in which rent enters, I am speaking of raw products.

Into the cost of raw agricultural products labor largely enters. It is safe to say that seven-eights of such products can be called labor. (See table V).

Thus, raw products=⅞ labor+⅛ rent, profit and interest.

Now, when these raw products go through the process of manufacture and transportation, wherein the vast amount of addition to cost is profit and interest, by use of machinery and money, which bear a much greater proportion than labor, the cost will be found to represent not over three-fifths, or sixty per cent. of labor. Thus Adam Smith says:

"In reality high profits tend much more to raise the price of work than high wages. If in the linen manufacture, for example, the wages of the different working people, the flax dressers, the spinners, the weavers, etc., should all of them be advanced two pence a day, it would be necessary to heighten the price of linen only by a

number of two pence equal to the number of people that
had been employed about it, multiplied by the number
of days during which they had been so employed. That
part of the price of the commodity which resolved itself
into wages would, through all the different stages of
the manufacture, rise only in arithmetical proportion to
the rise of wages. But if the profits of all the different
employers of these working people should be raised five
per cent., that part of the price of the commodity which
resolves itself into profit would, through all the different
stages of manufacture, rise in geometrical proportion to
the rise of profit. The employers of the flax dresser
would, in selling his flax, require an additional five per
cent. upon the whole value of the material and wages,
which he advanced to his workmen. The employers of
the spinners would require an additional five per cent.,
both upon the advanced price of the flax and upon the
wages of the spinners. And the employers of the weavers
would require a like five per cent., both upon the advanced price of the linen yarn and upon wages of the
weavers. In raising the price of commodities, the rise
of wages operates in the same manner, as simple interest
does in the accumulation of debt. The rise of profit
operates like compound interest. Our merchants and
master manufacturers complain much of the bad effect
of high wages in raising the price, and thereby lessening
the sale of their goods, both at home and abroad; they
say nothing of the bad effect of high profit. They are
silent regarding the pernicious effects of their own gains.
They complain only of those of other people.

The large addition of price, therefore, which
appear between raw products and finished products, is mostly profit and interest. Thus, a

yard of cotton cloth, which as cotton costs two
cents of labor, appears, as rent, profit and interest, four cents, and labor two cents, or gross
cost to the consumer—six cents, or 66 per cent.
R.+P.+I. and 33 per cent. labor. A sack of
flour has about 60 per cent. of labor and about
40 per cent. of R.+P.+I. It is safe to assume
that, if 12½ per cent. is the amount of labor in
raw products, not over 60 per cent. of cost will
be labor in finished products. Now, these finished products are the real return, or pay, which
the producer of raw products gets as his pay for
rent, wages and the use of his capital. He cannot eat wheat or wear wool.

Now, to see how the producer of raw products
comes out at the end of distribution, by examining the subjoined tables, it will be seen one
man's labor in farming one hundred and thirty-
four acres is represented as follows:

He receives as wages..$391.92
He received as rent, profit and interest................ 60.38
                                                        ————
    Total...$452.30

Now he receives in exchange finished products, which are composed as follows:

R., P. and I., 40 per cent.....................................$180.92
Wages—labor 60 per cent.................................... 271.38

Or, in other words, the R. P. I. in the finished

products absorbs not only all his own profits, all his interest, all the rent (with which Mr. George finds so much fault), but takes out of his wages $120.54, which goes to augment the profit or interest of somebody else. Thus Ricardo's law of rent stops too short to find out where distribution ends or determine wages or anything else.

This demonstration utterly does away with the theory of rent as now scientifically held by most writers upon this subject, who follow in the wake of Ricardo. Facts had already demonstrated that none of the necessary conclusions which result from the law were true. That wages did not go down, as Ricardo says they must; that prices did not go up, as Ricardo says they must; that land does not absorb its product, as Mr. George says it must; in short, that the law was no law, or rather there was another power or influence which they had not discovered, which overruled the law and rendered it neugatory. This is by this demonstration made plain. The law of profit and interest overrides and utterly destroys all conclusions usually supposed to depend upon this law. The attraction of gravitation brings water to the earth. We do not, therefore, conclude that all water is

found on the earth; other powers carry it back
and scatter it through the atmosphere. The patent
error in the Ricardo rent theory is in the assumption that there is but one rate of agricultural profit, and in entirely overlooking the fact
that interest on money is collected before rent,
or out of it. Agricultural profit varies from zero
to interest on money. Strictly speaking no rent
can be paid for land or economic rent arise until
profit has covered all direct and indirect interest
and paid profit equal to interest. Hence, land
may be poor to any degree that it brings the
lowest wages and 1, 2 or 3 per cent. profit on capital and yet have no economic rent—the difference in natural powers, over wages being absorbed by profit and interest, and they the
cause of low wages and not rent.

In a slight degree rent may influence agricultural wages, yet when this influence is thrown
into the great vortex of production and the general average of wages from other and independent causes, is felt, there remains no perceptible
influence upon wages from economic rent. As I
have again and again said, I make no reference
to the common use of the term as pay for the
use of buildings, houses or grounds for other
than productive purposes, as all such things are

governed by the law of profit and not rent; nor
do I refer to the effect of the draught upon production, commonly called rent, in any country
where the law of competition is countervailed by
monopolistic laws or customs, such as exist in
all European countries. Laws which prevent
the natural law of acquisition, like laws of primo-
geneture, or laws of entail, or such as give special
right to land owners as the privilege of voting
or holding office, and which has a tendency to
give a special price to land above that which
comes from its natural and indestructible powers,
are and do constitute the basis of aristocracy.
The power thus given to land to absorb the products of labor and produce poverty is one of
monopoly, created by law, and not the power of
economic rent.

CHAPTER II.

_____

Profit and the Law of Profit.

_____

A part of the return of production which by
right accrues to the owner of capital for its
use in production.

_____

All production is usually credited to labor.
From the prominence given to labor in the usual
discussions of this subject it has grown to be a
common idea that labor produces all wealth.
Experience proves this to be far from the truth.
The applied forces and powers of nature used in
driving machinery constitute the greater portion
of physical exertion which results in production.
The exertion which man contributes is largely
that of mental force and acquired skill in direct-
ing the agencies of nature. Even when it becomes necessary to exert the physical powers of
man, the agencies of capital intervene and al-

ways render this power more effective. The result of this contribution of physical energy by tools and machinery is a large increase of the acquisition of wealth, and is one of the causes of profit.

The gross amount of this increase cannot be called profit. Capital, like all other wealth, is constantly consumed, only in a different way. It is worn out and destroyed in use. A certain amount of the increase above spoken of must constantly be used to replace this consumption; a certain portion must go to pay insurance and taxes, which are a proper charge to replacement of capital, being the means of affording it protection and security. This comes out of the gross earnings of capital before we can compute net profit. Also, with all dealers who, by collecting and handling capital, serve the convenience of the community, such as middlemen and merchants, who add a certain percentage to their goods, which is to cover not profit alone, but the replacement of waste, insurance, transportation, wages and interest on money. Profit is the net gain after taking out all such expenses. All these and rent are added to the price of the product and collected in the cost to the consumer. So, when I speak of profit, I mean the sum which

is left to the producer for a return for the use of
capital—something added to value in form or
place capable of ministering to desire.   This is
the view taken by the best authorities on political economy.   Adam Smith says of revenue:
"That derived from stock by the person who
manages or employs it is called profit.   Capital
is increased by parsimony."   He also says that
the motive to parsimony and the increase of
capital is profit.   This idea, as expressed by
Simonidi, is, that abstainence is the means of
storing capital, and the motive to abstainence is
the increase gained thereby, or profit

Adam Smith wrote nearly one hundred years
ago.   Wonders wrought in productive modes
have, in this period, changed the whole condition of society, and the increased supplies to
meet necessities has rendered what might be considered profligacy then, abstainence now.   We
accordingly find later writers (Mill and Bastiat)
stating that while profit is the motive, the real
"cause of profit is that laborers produce more
than is required for their support;" that the surplus of production, not required for rent, interest
or wages, is profit.   Writers upon the ethics of
government have often questioned the right of
the owners of capital to receive this return, and

strong prejudice has been excited against capitalists, by reason of the claim, that capital could justly receive only replacement, and labor was entitled to all the balance of production. Numberless discertations have been written, both pro and con, among which are the elaborate defence of profit (he calls it interest) by Henry George, and the like defence of interest and profit by Bastiat. It seems to me, however, that one simple illustration by Ricardo had long before settled the whole question of the foundation of profit, and its justice. I use the illustration, but not Ricardo's words.

A farmer expends labor and capital upon land, and gets a return, say, 5 net. He now tiles and fertilizes the land (this is simply adding capital), and by the same labor gets 6 net. He now buys improved machinery, and by the same relative labor gets 7 net. Rent is the same, interest the same; labor the same. To whom, if not to him, does the 1 and 2 belong, and what are they, if not additions to his wealth, or capital? And what are they to be called, if not profit? Wherever capital is used, no one will continue to use the same and produce for others, for less than they can produce for themselves, whether upon land, or the products of land, and so capital can always demand as profit, an amount above the same which will induce labor to store, or replace it. It hardly seems possible, that any one can deny that this return is just and equitable, who holds to the right of individual freedom, and the consequent right to the ownership of that which his own hand has created.

Mr. George, however, says that the cause of profit ("interest") "arises from the increase which the reproductive forces of nature, and, in effect, analigous capacity of exchange gives to capital." Barring the fact, that Mr. George always confounds interest and profit, and that his definition of profit makes a close shave upon his definition of rent, it comes to just the same general conclusion, and it may be stated as the unanimous verdict, that profit is just, and an increase, a surplus of production, which goes to the owner of capital as a return to him for the use of capital in productive modes. While it is universally admitted that the surplus is profit, and that it is just, I must always insist upon two facts being kept in mind:

1st. That the reward of profit is not the only motive for storing capital.

2nd. That parsimony is not the source of capital.

The controlling motive for storing capital is necessity. This preceeds all other motives. Without capital man would perish. They must apply their labor in order to procure bread, and their labor cannot be of avail without capital. Sustenance, they must have, whether anything is left for increase, as profit or not. As I have shown before, the vast majority of capital works for little more than replacement, and much of it at the margin of cultivation. Probably there is no more misleading nonsense, in all political economy, than the idea, growing out of the confounding interest and profit, than, as Adam Smith says, "Profit is about equal to interest." If the profit of the agriculturist was equal to the interest on money, there would be a surprise-party for the inhabitants of the globe in about one hundred and fifty years. Let the stock hogs alone, of the farms, increase at 7 per cent., compounded for one hundred and fifty years, they would be about the only inhabitants of the globe. They would stand one deep over all the land, and a large share of the moon would have to be rented to furnish them standing room. In a very few trades and localities profit is made equal to interest. In all others, capital and labor work for just about replacement. So when we read in economic treatise, that manufacturers and dealers must make wages of superintendence, interest and replacement of capital, the statement would be correct if changed to read: "They must make wages, replace capital, and profit equal to interest, if they can." If they make enough to pay interest, and half as much on their own capital, they do well.

The real source of capital increase, or of increase of wealth (both may be profit), will, I think, be found in the increased capacity to produce by means of machinery, by a further division of labor, by increased facilities of commerce, so as to equalize values, and reduce rent. Whatever increases the amount of production over the demands of society, adds a proportion to profit, though how, and to what extent, modified by interest and wages, remains to be seen.

CHAPTER III.

Interest

Is a "derivitive revenue," derived from the power of money to store capital, and hence the power to absorb whatever profit such capital makes in production. What is a just interest, what inflation, and what construction, defined.

The subject of interest in no treatise, of which I have any knowledge, is discussed separately from profit. Its genesis, amount, ethics, influence, and effects are all discussed in common, as one thing, with profit. The most casual observation should convince anyone of the utter folly of such a blunder. Money is not consumed in an economic sense. Its use, or failure to use it, produces nothing. Therefore, under the principle of abstainence, it is not saved, or under the surplus of its production interest is not attained. Plant it and water it, as Mr. George suggests, apply any or all "the reproductive forces of nature to it," and no extra dollars appear. Transport it, or use it in exchange, and its value is not increased (as is capital), but usually of less value by exchange, in the price of transportation. Taken in any view in which money is presented by political economists, interest is little less than robbery, as Mr. George remarks. Indeed, we find that while capital always expects profit, money in all the great work of facilitating distribution, for which it was originally invented, thus aiding in the division of labor, expects, and, in fact, receives no interest. It is, then, an exchange of equivalents; of value, for wealth, for which it pays. It is only when money is used to represent credit, or in storing capital, that money commands interest. As I have already shown, it is not a natural thing, but acquired. The potential power given to money, by the State, to extinguish indebtedness, carries with it the command of wealth, of capital, and all the natural use and function of capital under the natural law of competition. It is, therefore, a derivitive power, derived from the State, the direct action of government to interfere with the laws of competition. In this, and this alone, arises the power to demand interest, and all the questions, therefore, which are commonly mooted, of the justice of interest, refers back at once to the question of what is a just, and natural exercise of this prerogative of government. That there is a dim, vague, but widespread and universal impression, that interest is robbery, grows out of the failure of economists to clearly apprehend and state the just meets and bounds of interest. That all nations feel that interest is not a natural thing, or grounded in the same principles as profit, is proved by the futile attempts to regulate it, or curb the rapacity of money-loaners, by usury laws. Why not curb production by law, and regulate profit in the same way? Why not say that a man shall not raise but 18 bushels of wheat upon an acre? Just as much sense in one as in the other, if both are based upon natural justice. They are not. One is natural, and the other artificial.

In order to ascertain whether a law, creating money, has been exercised in accordance with natural justice, the law of equal competion, so as to produce a just interest, and if not, to determine what ought to be done to produce such results, it will be necessary to examine the effect of interest upon society, in its relations to all the factors of production

We have seen, that interest on money is collected out of profit, or rent, or both; that it is collected out of the consumer, by being added to cost. The first startling thing which presents itself, is, that interest, while it conforms to profit at the highest point of production, it is not paid by such profit, but is charged up on the products of industry, and collected out of the labor, or rent, or profit of all classes of community, whether working at the margin, or above.

To illustrate: Farming communities work their capital and lands, and get the average of production, say 2 net. A capitalist sees a favorable location, to make agricultural implements, in a large farming community, and having $10,000, puts up works for this purpose. Needing more money, he borrows $10,000, at 6 per cent. interest, and purchasing stock pays therefore with the money. He has now to pay each year $600, as interest upon the money. He adds enough to the price of the implements, which he sells, and collecting the money from the purchasers, pays it over to the money loaner. The interest is not paid by him, but by the rent, wages, profit and interest in the goods. That is, interest comes out of the profit of all who consume, and these are necessarily mostly producers, from the margin to the highest point of production, or in other words, out of the average of capital increase. In this particular case, out of the profit of 2 per cent., comes interest of 6 per cent. and profit of 6 per cent.

Thus, the first injustice, in any country where the supply of money is regulated so as to keep interest above the average increase of wealth, is that it gives to the holders of money, as a natural sequence of law, the power to take out of production a larger share of the product than is made by the average of capital, and is a monopoly to this extent.

See again: In this same illustration, let the circumstances be changed, so as to reduce interest to 3 per cent., or about the average of profit, and what would be the result? The amount before charged up, and collected as interest, would be divided by two and taken off from agricultural implements, and the price reduced accordingly, leaving this amount in the hands of the purchaser. Some other man with $10,000, seeing our capitalist still making 6 per cent. upon his capital, will build another factory alongside of him, and make agricultural implements, the

motive for storing money, being less than the
motive for storing capital; and both would, by
competition, be compelled to approximate to 3
per cent. profit; and so would the miller up the
valley, and the cotton mills just below, and the
railroads, and all capital stored by money. This
would again reduce prices to the farmer, the
laborer, the wage-worker, and leave in his hands
the profit, and interest, which, by unjust operation of law, is taken away from them. It would
further indefinitely increase the amount of capital and demand for labor.

The second injustice of interest above the
average of production, is that it contracts the
power of storing capital, and hence the power of
labor to produce, creates a ruinous competition
between laborers, and destroys all other health-
ful competition.

Take the same illustration again: The natural
consequence of the increase of production by
lowering interest to 3 per cent., under ordinary
circumstances in society, would make a largely
increased demand for money to transact ordinary
business, and would lessen the amount for loan,
and raise interest. The consequence would be,
that as interest raised to 4 per cent., the capitalist would be compelled to raise prices, or pay the

4 per cent. of interest out of his 3 per cent. of profit. This would contract production, and capital would be turned into money, the motive being greater to store money than capital. The same thing is often done by the holders of money, it being a thing which does not waste or decay like capital, by making it artificially scarce, thus compelling men, who are in need, to pay higher rates than a just return for money.

This is the third injustice of maintaining any system of money which keeps interest above the average of profit. It gives the power of expending and contracting the profits of capital, the power which makes and breaks the whole community. The increase of interest comes out of profit, and decreases the motive for storing capital.

Again take the same example: The $10,000 thus loaned to store capital is not used in the sense of using wealth. It is simply parted with. In a week or a month it gets back into the bank, and is loaned again at 6 per cent., and again employs men and stores capital, and again in a few weeks it is loaned to go through the same process. Loans and discounts show that all money is thus loaned, from two to three times, at an average of from two to three times the average increase of capital.

This is the fourth arraignment which the law of justice and free competition brings against any law or system of laws, which renders money so scarce as to almost compel the geometrical increase of the non-producing factor of distribution out of the slow and laborious accumulation of labor and capital. This condition is a necessary sequence of the nature and power of money, and is neither unjust or wrong, if the average of interest is made to conform to profit, as then the new capital stored by money, and which is really the representative of the credit given by money, would produce to the possessor sufficient to pay the interest, and society would not be injured.

The normal condition of interest, under just government, is the average increase of wealth, as this is the average of profit which accrues from its use; and any arrangement or want of arrangement by government, by which interest can be demanded for a greater amount than this, is a direct interference of the state to do an injustice; is in contravention of the laws of competition and a direct violation of the principles of equity. Every atom of interest above this normal line is an inflation of interest by a contraction of credit, a gratuitous give-away by society—pure wind.

Here, then, is the explanation of the term of inflation and contraction; terms so commonly banded about in political writings, but never explained.

Any condition of money, which leaves the surplus of money for loan so scarce that a greater interest can be demanded for it than the average of the profits of capital, is contraction, and the reverse is inflation. The usual condition of all countries is contraction of the volume of money, This condition, as I have shown in three ways, tends at every stage above the normal condition of interest to stop or prevent the storing of capital; to this extent destroys the power of production; throws labor out of employment by placing the motive for storing the non-producing factor above the producing factor; in short, it renders it impossible by operation of law, or want of law for any other condition to exist, than that in which just as much wealth shall be in the hands of the few as possible consistent with the balance continuing to produce. All the shallow pretense of political writers, that money is but a form of wealth, is thus shown in its cruel deformity.

CHAPTER IV.

WAGES.

The pay for human exertion—always forced to
a minimum. The means by which this is
accomplished—means by which it can be
prevented. Natural wages are the whole
product of labor, except enough to compensate for storing capital.

Labor is about the only thing in society which
is freely exercised under, and controlled by, the
law of competition. Every laborer is liable to
be a competitor with every other, and, for some
unexplained reason, labor is always pressing on
the market. Naked, man comes into the world.
At maturity, unless by some good fortune he
comes into the possession of the savings of
others, he has but his own hands to depend
upon to supply his wants. Idle lands he sees

everywhere capable of supplying every necessity, but upon investigation he finds that with
the best appliances and application, after supplying the wants and necessities of humanity,
there is left but a little over 2 per cent. of the
return upon the expenditure necessary to avail
oneself of its natural powers.   He must procure
capital to make his labor available upon this
land, or in any direction, and so he looks for it,
and finds that after replacement and all incidents
of capital, and making return to labor over and
above the same, supplies a return of not much
above 3 per cent.   Should he go to some neigh-
bor and propose to borrow a horse and plow and
seed, or money to purchase the same, and offer
to pay what capital produces, he will be told that
money is close, is worth 6 per cent., 7 per cent.
or 8 per cent., and it being pretty evident that
he cannot pay 6 per cent. out of a gain of 3 per
cent., he does not purchase, and the land lies
idle, and another man jostles with his fellow
laborers for a place to earn bread.   This jostle
for a place to earn bread has gone on since civilization commenced.   Henry VIII. hung 70,000
vagrants, men seeking to work for bread.   The
poor houses of all Europe are full of them.   The
most progressive and prosperous nation, so-

called civilized nations, have them; when not
very plenty they are called loafers and vagrants;
when plenty, tramps.

The political economists finds them, and becomes so used to them that he comes to consider them a natural phenomenon—a necessary
outgrowth of order of nature. Thus originates
the theory of the "pressure of population" of
Malthus, which, as it wained, was followed by
that of Ricardo of necessary poverty. This
theory, so highly endorsed by the eminent Mr.
Mill, as that he calls it the "pons assinorum" of
political economy, and recommends as the *ultima
thule* of labor to restrict the production of children. Just as though children were not necessary to make men, and men necessary to labor,
and labor necessary to produce capital and
wealth, any one of whom can produce ten times
as much as he consumes. The inventor of this
remedy certainly ought to have a patent on it.

Having kicked the props out from under this
bridge, which was the seeming cause of all labor's
woes, I may be pardoned if I totally repudiate
all such theories, and replace them with one
which conforms to the dictates of reason, and is
the necessary outgrowth of the relation of wages
to the other factors of distribution. It will not

be found to be a natural phenomenon, but the result of social adjustments; the result of ignorance or design, which can under no circumstances produce other consequences.

The condition in which civilized society has always existed since the invention of money has been one of total ignorance of its relations and functions. Every conceivable form of money has been used and made, and are now made and used. Quantities of from $5 to $50 per capita, with interest from 3 per cent. to 50 per cent., have existed, and do now exist, with seeming, absolute disregard of its relations, or whether it has any relations to production. What should be money, character, quality, functions, quantity, etc., has been the grand guess of all ages.

One class of society, without knowing or probably caring about ulterior consequences, have always had in view the fact that, if money was scarce, they could have high interest and live without labor upon the labor of others. Partially through such influences, but more especially from the different views of supposed authority upon this subject, the volume of money has always been in a condition of contraction. That is, in all countries and at all times, it has been so scarce that the average interest has far exceeded the average make of capital, out of which it has to be paid. This gives into the hands of the venders of money, as I have stated under the head of interest, to take all profit and rent and the large share of the wages of the great bulk of society. But this is not all. Capital is stored by the slow accumulations of labor upon natural agents and products, and also by the use of money or credit, under certain conditions which I have explained. What interest takes as above is the slow accumulations of labor, leaving it without increase of capital to employ labor; but what is worse, it absolutely cuts off all motive to store capital to be used upon agents, which will produce less than profit equal to interest; for if interest is so high that land or other opportunities will not pay net profit equal to interest, there would be no voluntary demand to store capital to use such opportunities, though the earth was teeming with food and clothing and comforts ready to be brought forth for man's use. And should it so occur that at or near the average of interest, on account of the increased power of production, it were possible to supply all wants of society, leaving out a part of labor, such labor might go starve or hang itself. It would have no other alternative.

The manner in which contraction affects wages are :

1st. It gives to interest and profit a larger share of the products of labor than would naturally go to them.

2nd. It cuts off all voluntary storage of capital, necessary to be used, to make land available below the margin of interest; thus throwing out labor from making capital for such purpose, and also from the use of opportunities upon poorer land.

3rd. As a consequence it brings a large class of society always into idleness, who stand as competitors in the market with other laborers, and thus gives capital the power to coerce labor to any wages at which men will work.

The most powerful motive which actuates men in society exists to so maintain interest, that the non-producing few, can absorb the products of labor and capital. This motive is to satisfy desire with the least exertion. It is most perfectly gained, if production can be controlled so as to produce idleness on the part of many, forcing labor lower and lower, enabling capital to make larger and larger gains. Its only limit is the endurance of the producer.

The condition in which the laborer is thus placed can be illustrated farther by examining the manner in which wages are taken. When I speak of wages I refer to all who work as wage workers, or as managers of capital in the production of wealth.

"The real pay of the laborer is the product of labor," so says Adam Smith. Although this is usually paid in money, the money is but the representative of something which money distributes, something which satisfies desire. The production of one man is the consumption of another. Real wages are, therefore, the product of his own labor. The price of all consumable commodities resolve themselves into R., W., P. and I. In any country where high interest and high profit prevail the relative proportion of I. and P. are high. When we recollect what Adam Smith says of profit and interest, how they are computed in all products, over and over again, it is safe to conclude in the United States that a fair estimate of the cost of supplies which labor gets for wages would be—

Rent—5,+P. 15,+I. 20 and wages 60=100.

The laborer, when he gets his $2 for his day's

labor and purchases flour, exchanges his $2 of labor for $1.20 of labor and 80 cents of (R., I. and P.) There is no escape from this. The interest on $3,000,000,000 of railroad bonds, and profit on as much more stock, are figured into carrying rates and added to cost, and collected in every home from hovel to palace. Profit of all manufacturers, and the interest on borrowed money used by them, profits of all common carriers and the interests they pay, discounts of all banks, in short, all profit, interest and rent, go into the price of coffee, sugar, clothing and the like, and are collected almost wholly out of the vast many who labor for wages, or with their capital, at or near the margin. The law is as the law of the Medes and Persians, as inexorable as fate.

This is not the natural condition of wages. The natural condition is one in which labor should receive the whole product of exertion, except sufficient to induce the storing of capital ; the small return necessary to induce labor to turn from one employment to another, or about the increase of wealth Should the surplus of money to loan be increased so as to reduce interest and keep it there, the entire relations of labor would then be natural. Interest would exact no more than the amount produced by capital, out of which it was paid, and by it stored; profit by competition would drop to a level with interest, and the equation of wages would represent something as follows.

R. 2,+I. 6,+P. 5,+W. 87,=100.

The flour, which, at 6 per cent. interest cost $2, would, at 3 per cent. interest, cost $1.46, and wages would relatively be 30 per cent. higher.

The reduction of interest, would further open up all opportunities for labor, make a motive at all times to store capital rather than remain idle, and all labor being employed would give a greater demand for products as fast as produced. Instead of labor pressing for a place to earn bread, capital would compete for labor, and thus again raise wages. Instead of the whole surplus product of labor being concentrated in the hands of a few, it would remain in the hands of those who produced it, augmenting the capital, which could employ labor, and production could go on until all desires became satisfied, and men would rest from groveling care, and be enabled to enjoy the higher walks of social and intellectual life.

CHAPTER V.

The Solution.

The foregoing explanation of the relation of the factor of distribution, to the factors of production, made to solve the various problems, which are vexing and threaten the destruction of society, to wit: Panics, over-production, the tramp, the pauper and the millionaire.

I have now examined and grouped all the factors which enter into production and distribution. I have discovered their relation and effects upon each other, which result from social adjustment existing in society. I have shown what ought to be the result of their natural relations, existing freely under the law of competition and untrammelled by maladjustments of society. As all writers have heretofore constantly confounded these relations, and rendered their conclusions unreliable of a necessity, so when given their proper places and relations, the conclusions drawn ought to bear the weight of mathematical certainty. Happily this proves itself to be a fact. Tested by these explanations, theory and fact for once agree; reason and political economy are in accord; ambiguities and riddles, which have vexed the brightest minds, are made plain; doubts and uncertainties which have made vascillation and hesitancy a prominent feature in legislation vanish, and the way indicated by which government, with perfect freedom, based upon justice, can, and I believe, can only be maintained.

The natural order in production is that land is worthless without labor. All objects which satisfy human desire are the fruit of labor. Capital is essential to make labor available. The natural order in compensation, therefore, is labor, capital, land. When labor is exerted upon land freely, I have shown, after absolute necessities are supplied, *i. e.*, when labor and capital are voluntarily exercised upon land, it arises from a motive, the motive of procuring the surplus or profit. That labor will be exerted in one or another direction, in proportion as the motive is greater in storing capital or in storing wealth for destructive consumption. It is the natural outgrowth of the motive which controls all men, the tendency to satisfy their desires with the least amount of labor. And hence, so long as there is no stronger controlling motive, and this motive of ordinary profit exists, all necessary capital will be stored to employ all labor to the extent of all opportunities, natural or created— the limit being labor and opportunities, and the whole product going to labor, except the small portion necessary to divert labor from one employment to another; and when land is appropriated, wages of labor employed thereon, modified by the almost imperceptible difference in natural powers of productiveness.

This is the condition when money appears upon the scene Here comes an agent supplied by the state which produces nothing, but brings a return, which, without labor on its part, supplies all the necessities and desires of man, which never rests, rots or decays, which represents all accumulations of wealth, all credits, and has the power to store wealth—more desirable than any form of wealth, because it commands all wealth and labor and opportunities, and can, therefore, always command the highest.

The man who has capital must use it or it be-

comes worthless. Its employment requires hand
and brain, brings chances of business, risk of loss
by fire or flood, and is subject to constant waste
and depletion. Money can wait. Without labor
or chances, its possessor rests in ease, while
the sweating, toiling millions wring from the
bosom of unwilling nature his comfortable living.

From the very nature and condition under
which money originates, there has always been a
chronic condition of contraction of the money of
all countries   Made of all kinds of material,
supplemented by various devices, invented
often under stress of necessity, its quantity has
always been like the temperature varying as
every wind set in the atmosphere of society.
Through all these variations at no time has a
money, which maintained its representative value,
been made in such quantities as to conform to a
just interest.   Some nations have approximated
to this, others have disregarded it altogether,
and others have made it the subject of caprice
altogether.   The tendency of money is always,
but especially in a progressive country, to contraction.

1st.   Because the material out of which money
has been freely made by nations is always limited.
The metals, gold and silver, one or the other are

and have been in all ages the only metals out of which money could be made at will, and never at any time have they been plenty enough to supply one-tenth of the actual needs of the money of the world, so as to reduce interest to an equality with the factors of production, and thus render justice between man and man.

2nd.   The very moment you get an established quantity of money in a country, and business adjusted to this quantity, population and business must grow, if there is any room to grow.   This creates a demand for money in the increase of the products to be exchanged, and the credit needed to store new capital.   Now, no nation has ever provided, except France, I believe, at one time, anything to obviate this difficulty.   Various devices have been created, intending to meet this difficulty, but they have all failed, such as our national banking system, the Bank of England, and the like, but they do not go far enough, and for the very good reason, which is also a reason for the contraction of the currency, viz.:

3rd.   Money is not a thing created by labor, or increased as you increase capital, or produced as you produce wheat or oats.   Those who deal in money, and could increase the quantity and keep interest at 4, 5 or 6 per cent., are just as

well served, and a little better, if money is in demand at 7 or 8 per cent. They are compelled to
do just one-half the business to make the same
money, at 8 per cent. as at 4, and to leave the
question of quantity in their hands, is the Fable
of the Fox and Stork over again. This I say
without any discourtesy to the profession. They
are not compelled to pull the public chestnuts
out of the fire, or to discommode themselves, to
do a good turn to labor and capital, if labor and
capital are so negligent of their own.

4th. The direct action of classes of individuals, who understand the effect of the increase of
money, as seen in demonitizing one or the other
metals, when it is likely to reduce interest.
Various reasons are often given, but the true
reason why superhuman exertion was made to
demonitize silver lately, was because the quantity
was liable to increase the power of labor and
capital, by decreasing interest.

5th. With all this the condition could not
exist, for any length of time, were it not for the
demoralization of public sentiment, occasioned
by the erronious teachings of political economy.
These teachings, as I have shown, based upon
ambiguous foundations, leave upon the public
mind an impression that the public has little in-

terest in the question of money. No knowledge has, therefore, been imparted, that the very life and existence of society depends upon money, and hence they allow it to be controlled by those whose interests are antagonistic, and whose bread is their blood. So that in all pretended civilizations, there is constituted by law this factor of money, which brings in a new phaze in the field of distribution, and is the open sesame to the various conditions in society which we are discussing.

I propose to examine and apply these principles, in detail, to the conditions to be explained.

BUSINESS DEPRESSIONS AND PANICS.

All business depressions and panics are directly accounted for by the varying conditions of money, and are especially noticeable in their effects as resulting from the law of the supply of money, as governed and controlled in two different modes.

1st. Take a progressive country like the United States, and any period at which business has settled to the then present supply of money; new lands are constantly being opened up, requiring new capital; factories must constantly go up to supply this capital; new demand constantly to store such capital; private credit stretched to its utmost; public credit (money) not increasing in proportion, interest goes up; business which at 5 per cent. was profitable, at 6 becomes less so; business which was being done nearer the margin becomes profitless; all business on capital stored at 3 per cent. or 4 per cent., at 6 or 7 per cent. becomes valueless, as all profit goes to interest; production ceases at the extremities, because high profit and high interest carry consumable products higher and higher in price; demand ceases; railroad traffic falls off; failures are recorded by the dozen; mills shut down; stagnation everywhere; men idle; money so scarce at business centres that from 10 to 20 per cent. a day is demanded for its use; banks cease to loan, proceed to call in discounts; money congests in the centres; reserves of banks get plethoric; after awhile interest drops a little; mills start; labor goes to work, and goes through the same round over and over again.

The second mode, is when the contraction of credit is not relative, but the direct action of government in contracting the money of the country, or where it is done by the exportation of the money, resulting in a like contraction. It occurs in all countries, but especially in one

which depends entirely upon an exportable commodity, like gold or silver, for its money volume.
It was the direct cause of the periodic panics,
which came and went as the tide, bringing devastation and destruction in their wake, prior to
the present system of money, based, in part,
upon the wealth and labor of the country. Gold
and silver were then the basis of money, and
private credit based upon these, and redeemable,
or supposed to be so, in this kind of money.
This credit, issued without any reference to the
demand of business, solely to the end of private
gain, soon set the wheels of commerce and manufacture in motion, and the best lands which could
afford to store capital, at the highest rate of interest, were occupied. Production carried on at
such disadvantage, gave it into the hands of any
nation who so arranged interest, as to carry on
production, at a low rate, to undersell all articles
of manufacture, into which profit and interest
largely enter as an ingredient of price, and thus
carry away the gold and silver in exchange for
their cheaper products. Money thus became
scarcer and scarcer; private credit greater and
greater; interest draughts greater and greater,
and when the time came that payments must be

made, this private credit, based upon nothing, collapsed.

The history of all panics and business depressions of all countries will show that contraction, relative or actual, has caused every such panic in the history of civilization; that on their recurrence again and again, some new scheme of wildcat money has always been patched up to ruin the next generation. Common sense shows anyone, that had money been kept at an interest, at or near the average increase of wealth, there could be no panic, because there could be no general failure to meet obligations, the wealth realized from capital stored on the average, meeting all obligations.

And so the mystery, which hangs around the words

OVER PRODUCTION.

fades away as the light of these truths is turned upon it. Whenever, in the course of events, it so happens that by the increase of productive power, from the increase of mechanical appliances, three-fourths of any people are able to produce for the whole, and interest is maintained so high that the greater proportion of production using capital voluntarily stored by money, *i. e.*

for profit, is carried on above the average increase
of wealth, the remaining one-fourth may stand
still, though opportunities below this average of
interest may be as thick as huckleberries. The
graneries and warehouses of those producing
will be crowded with goods and merchandise,
simply because by this abnormal condition the
balance of society is barred from using its labor,
and of course has nothing, or comparatively
nothing, to exhange for products, which are
everywhere wanting a market. This is over
production. When interest is so high as to
necessitate capital being used only in connection
with high opportunities, barring out the storing,
or using capital in less productive fields, and yet
producing enough for all, and this is the exact
commençement and birth of that condition of

EXTREME POVERTY: THE ORIGIN OF THE TRAMP.

Under the foregoing circumstances, suppose a
man has land which will produce, say 3 per cent.
net, and has no capital; to use his labor he must
buy capital on credit, or borrow money and buy.
He produces 3 per cent. and pays 6 per cent. interest, or in other words, he just makes wages.
Now interest rises to 7 per cent.; he must take
out of his wages the 1 per cent. to pay this extra

to interest.   One bad harvest and he is a beggar.
And what of him who has not land or capital
when such a time arrives.   Strong, vigorous,
capable, he stands in society an absolutely useless thing; his labor not needed by others; opportunities to make wages all around him, but
the means to use these opportunities held above
the possibility of his ever making return.   He is
just as absolutely barred out of production, by
the 'force of these artificial circumstances, as if
he was an absolutely naked man, standing on a
barren rock in mid-ocean.   He has only one advantage, he can beg or steal.   He sees around
him plenty, just beyond his reach; he hears the
laughter and mirth, and sees the sunlight which
brings joy to the bedecked hills, none of which
ever crosses the threshold of his soul; out of place
in the world, an Ishmaelite—hope dies, brooding discontent and hatred takes possession—he
is fermenting the blood of revolution.   And so
as natural as day succeeds day we find the vast
majority of the wealth in the hands of the few.

The contraction of credit contracts the power
of production, and creates a relation between different parts of production, that the return to all
capital stored at the ordinary rate of 2 and 3 per
cent. is absorbed by the profit of capital, and

money used at the top of production; or, in other
words, the quantity of money, like the balance
of a steam engine, makes use of all the higher
opportunities of production to draw to itself the
whole product of the community. Not simply
by drawing the extra percentage over ordinary
profit, but by actually curtailing production so
that a few can absorb the wealth and wages of
all. If one-sixth of the production of any country was done on interest of 6 per cent., and the
average profit was 1 per cent., the whole of the
surplus or profit would be in the hands of one-
sixth. They would produce nothing, but absorb
all.

Although the wisdom or the selfishness or the
ignorance of man has never shown what might
be the result, was the law of justice established
in regard to money, and its interest reduced and
kept at a rate which corresponds with the amount
of its advantage to society, yet we have occasional glimpses in history, when, as it were,
the vail was lifted, and we were permitted to
look into the vestibule of that glorious condition in the world when production should be
untrammeled by such injustice. There have
been some cases in history which show and
demonstrate the capacity of humanity to pro-

duce. Occasionally a political economist, in a
state of partial sanity on this subject, will give
testimony. Such is the case with Adam Smith,
"Wealth of Nations," book No. 2, chapter iv.

Here for once he keeps money and capital
separate, profit and interest separate as they
should be, and see how straight a story he tells:

" As the stock to be lent at interest increases the interest, or the price which must be paid for the use of that
stock, necessarily diminishes, not only from those general causes which make the market price of things commonly diminished as their quantity increases, but from
other causes which are peculiar to this particular case.
As capitals increase in any country the profits which can
be made by employing them necessarily diminish. It
becomes gradually more and more difficult to find within
the country a profitable method of employing any new
capital. There arises in consequence a competition between different capitals, the owners of the one endeavor-
ing to get possession of that employment which is occupied by another. But upon most occasions he can hope
to jostle that other out of this employment by no other
means, but by dealing upon more reasonable terms. He
must not only sell what he deals in somewhat cheaper,
but in order to get it to sell, he must sometimes too, buy
it dearer. The demand for productive labor by the increase of the funds which are destined for maintaining it
grows every day greater and greater. Laborers easily
find employment, but the owners of capital find it difficult to get laborers to employ. Then competition raises
wages of labor and sinks the profit of stock."

There you have it, when the great teacher

speaks without ambiguity of confounding money with capital or interest with profit. And the story runs, as money increases interest decreases, profit falls, prices fall; not rise (as Mr. Mill says); wages rise, or, in other words, the tendency of production is back to the normal condition, in which labor gets all the product except the minimum which would restore capital.

In this direction is the testimony of Mr. Hume, the eminent historian, who, after exhaustive review of society, sums up thus:

"Accordingly we find that in every kingdom into which money begins to flow in greater abundance than formerly, everything takes on a new face, labor and industry gain new life, the merchant becomes more enterprising, the manufacturer more diligent and skillful, and even the farmer follows his plow with more alacrity and attention. * * *

"The good policy of the government consists only in keeping if possible, still increasing, because by that means it keeps alive the spirit of industry in the nation and increases the stock of labor, in which consists all real power and riches."

These sentiments are the burden of scientific writings upon this subject, which I need not quote.

Mr. Mill tells us that with the increase of capital production could go on indefinitely until all labor was employed. The limit of the quantity of capital in any country can never be reached until you reach the limit of labor so long as interest is maintained below the average increase of wealth.

In concluding this part of the subject I desire to say that the scientific conclusions here deduced are in strict conformity to actual facts in the experience of business men.

Go into any community and inquire for the person who is reputed the man of wealth, and you will find that the man who commenced early, and continued to loan money. has prospered as well as the best.

Millionaires are not found among the producers of raw products, in which are mostly labor. They are found among manufacturers, middlemen, bankers; men who have not created the wealth they possess, but have, through the power of interest and profit, at the top of production, absorbed the makings of many thousand of their fellows. The lever which has lifted them to the heights, has on the other end the tens of thousands who have gone down to hard, half-requited toil, and many to misery and suffering. It is not a thing which is hidden any longer or a mystery. It is the natural outgrowth of injustice which can be written upon the tombs of nations.

"Interest above the average increase of wealth is a certain destruction of equality and of freedom."

"Governments are based upon justice or bayonets."

"Law in accordance with justice or a government of force."

BOOK III.

THE REMEDY.

CHAPTER I.

An analysis of other proposed remedies, showing that no one of them will correct existing
evils, or meet the requirements of justice.

Having now made plain the cause of the per-
sistence of poverty amidst a superabundance of
production and ever increasing power of production, it will be advisable to examine the various
remedies which have been suggested to ascertain if any one is adequate to correct the difficulty, and if not, wherein the failure is made apparent.

The first which naturally suggests itself is that
which is first in the order of society, has existed

since the commencement of civilization, and in
early society was a bar to unequal conditions.
It is called

CO-OPERATION,

and means an organization inside of advanced
civilization, in which the members labor for the
common good of each other, with common capital and division of results, whether profit or loss.
The history of such organizations may be written
in a few words. If they employ themselves in
the production of raw products, and make their
surplus exchanges with the outside world for
products, which contains a large amount of
profit and interest as an element of price, the society will live at the margin of cultivation, or at
or near the verge of poverty; no absolute desti-
tution, but scarcely any comforts, luxuries or accumulations. If they combine more and more
of manufacturing and other industries, in which
interest is added to cost, they will thrive, increase and live luxuriously if they choose. If
they combine the element which makes the
greatest draught upon society, issue their own
money, add to their exchanges interest and
profit, which costs nothing to get, they will become rich, powerful and prosperous. The great
co-operative societies of England, especially those

of Rochedale and London, the co-operative
building associations of Pennsylvania, and, in
fact, all such organizations which succeed, are
those which pay no interest and profit, which is
not compensated by interest and profit drawn
from without. Such societies cannot help suc-
ceeding under fair management, as their very
constitution secures a just division of proceeds,
and the average of production of all countries is
not only enough to insure comfort and plenty,
but is always increasing. These statements show
that the conditions are always limited in which
co-operative organizations can be maintained.
They must embrace a large range of production,
so as to embrace an average range of productive
employment, or, if small, a productive employment up to this average. Thus, if a community
of farmers should co-operate and have no advantage of manufacturing, the small average
profit of those who were successful would be divided with those who might fail, but they would
exchange their product, which contained mostly
labor, with the manufacturer, whose goods are
burdened with high interest and profit, and no
benefit would accrue. Their labor would go
where it now goes, in exchange partly for the
labor of others, partly for legitimate profit, and a

large share of it for wind. All profit above the average of production is something taken for nothing—a pure give-away by society, wind; so that co-operation can do no good only in limited areas, where they make the very few on the inside, on the average better off, but always at the expense of the outside, if any more successful than they. But I hear some one asking, then, why not

SOCIALISM,

an enlarged co-operation, in which all society is a stockholder; or, in other words, a government which organizes society so that the whole production shall be shared by all alike. Of this class are the systems advocated by Fourier and St. Simons. They are the opposite of individual freedom. In essence, they hold that individual powers and capacities should be held in obeyance to the common good. Carried out to its ultimate, it would hold, that individuals in society are responsible for the heredity, for the errors and deficiencies of the ancestry of other men. Co-operation is a voluntary act. Socialism, being designed to be universal, could not be voluntarily brought about so long as such ideas were repugnant, or rather, until men became utterly unselfish. If attained, therefore, it would be by coertion, and when so attained would destroy all motive for exertion, as the reward of such exertion would be merged in the public good. The natural tendency would be toward indolence and inertia, and the injustice would always face society, of compelling those who wrought, to be burdened with the lives of the thriftless and careless, and of placing those who were capable and successful, on a par with those who were dwarfs in physical and intellectual power.

Beside this, to be successful, socialism must embrace the whole earth, or that nation which adopts its teachings must remember to make arrangements, to so regulate its money, as to make interest on a par with the other nations of the earth, else those outside nations underselling its manufactures would break them down, and then by high profit and interest upon loaned credit, carry away the products of their labor, and leave them penniless, or compel them to equalize profit with industry, by prohibiting free intercourse.

The most advanced and philosophic minds see no hope for socialism (if there is any real desire), until men become utterly unselfish, and then of

a necessity no motive for it, or for government,
for that matter, for men could not suffer so long
as there was no motive to accumulate, as production would continue up to the supply of all necessities.

LABOR ORGANIZATIONS.

The effect of labor organizations, has, as a
usual thing, resulted in little good to those engaged in them. The trouble with the pay of
labor lays deeper down than the will or wish of
most employers. They are men like other men,
some of them with plenty of wolf in their com-
position, others with plenty of the milk of human
kindness. Thousands of employers would pay
better wages if they could. The draught of interest already alluded to, railroad discriminating
rates, profit and taxes, render it impossible to
pay greater wages and survive. When they
could, but will not pay greater wages, labor organizations seldom accomplish anything by trying to command wages, because, as I have shown,
and for the reason I have shown, there always
stands ready a large class of laborers to take
their vacant places, who have been, and always
are, pinched out by high interest and high profit,
so that no matter how unjust or oppressive

wages may have been, on the whole, the resort
to strikes has not been a paying business ; com-
puting time lost, extra expense of idleness, and
demoralization of the laborer, the extra pay
gained, seldom overcomes the loss in securing
the gain.

A curious fact connected with many strikes
which are constantly taking place, is the evident
want of information, respecting the real condition of production.   Any person who will take
the trouble to examine table viii. of the appendix to this work, will find that the total production of the United States for 1880, was $8,532,-
386,251 ; that this had to pay all waste, taxes,
interest, profit, rent and wages.   From division
"A" of that table, I have taken out the necessary charges for these expenses in society.   I
have then taken out the amount of the pay of
women, children and old men, and divided the
balance between the 12,986,111 men and youths
from 16 to 60 years of age, which the census
shows were engaged in labor and in the professions, and it gives $417.28 of the actual produc-
tion to each man per year, or $1.39 for each man
per day, if equally distributed.   I have again divided this total production between the 10,539,-
149 wage-workers, on the theory that they sup-

port the professional classes, and it gives to each
$523.76 per year, or $1.74½ per day of a year
of 300 days. Understand, this is on the basis of
present interest, and without any profit going to
capital. What it would be with lower interest is
another thing. But as long as the laborer works,
and votes for the present interest on money, he
is barking up the wrong tree when he strikes,
and has a salary of $1.74½ a day.

As long as he continues to exercise the real
power, and means to procure a just return and
just relations in society, *i. e* ; the elective franchise,
as he now does, and yet wants to compel an employer, to divide the results of his high profit
with him, he stands in the relation of a co-conspir-
ator with the very men who now destroy all the
real interest of both labor and capital.

I have shown as above, that all labor earns
only this small pittance. I have shown that the
reason is because labor is pinched out from work
and made to stand idle, producing nothing. I
I have shown that this is done through law, and
on purpose to accomplish this very end.

I have shown that as interest ascends, profit
must go down, or it must come out of wages.
That as interest goes up, it is and becomes more

profitable to stop work and throw men out, than
to keep them at work.

In any country, therefore, where men have the
elective franchise and go steadily forward voting
for men so ignorant of these truths, or whose
whole interest is in destroying production and
forcing wages to a minimum, and then strike for
more wages than their share of the whole production, what better are they than the monopo-
lists or the railroad wrecker.   Are they not con-
spiring to produce a condition in which the employer can exact a large amount of profit out of
the loss of fellow-labors, needle women, miners,
farm laborers, factory girls, and then want to
force a part of this public plunder, out of the employer, or, in other words, divide the swag?   I
say in all candor to laboring men their responsi-
bility does not end when they have turned off the
steam, or shut down the lathes ; nor in the lodge
when they have paid their dues ; they ought to
come up higher ; to get nobler and broader
views than those of individual wages.   The place
to strike is at the ballot box.   Every ballot cast
to perpetuate the system which now destroys the
interest of labor and capital alike, is wet with
tears of sorrow, which ought to scald and wither
the heart of the man who knowingly casts it.

Two or three things labor organizations can do :

1st.   They can, by a proper system of intelligence offices, bring employer and employed together so as to promote the interest of both.

2d.   By discussion and interchange of ideas, they can gain larger knowledge of the causes which lead to the depression of wages, and thus prepare themselves to make an intelligent demand of legislators for such laws as shall prevent any individual, or class of individuals, from becoming the sole owners of the product of labor and the life and destinies of the laborer, and if one legislature will not heed this demand, so unite the power of labor at the ballot box as to control legislation in the interests of justice.

3d.   Until such time as public sentiment is brought to fully understand the power and influence of scarce money and high interest, to drive labor from the field of production, such organizations might, by laying by small sums of money from the wages of its members, soon build establishments where labor combined with profit, and interest, would afford a reservoir into which idle labor could flow, until public sentiment could be aroused to strike down the means by which labor is now forced to a minimum.

ISSUE OF PAPER MONEY OR GREENBACKISM.

The leaders and promulgators of this theory teach that the way to remedy existing evils is to issue paper money. The foremost teachers and thinkers among this class, assert that as the money increases, the price of production increases, and the wages of labor in just the same proportion. That if money were doubled, wages would be doubled, and the price of products doubled. Now, as Adam Smith says, "the wages of labor are the products of labor." The logical outcome of this theory is, that the laborer is just as well off in one condition as in the other, for if this theory be true, when wages are $1.00 per day, and flour $1.00 per sack, when his wages rose with the increase of money to $2.00 per day flour would be $2.00 per sack. As the lobor scarcely ever has a surplus, what avail to him is such a condition? The real person under this theory who would be affected, would be the creditor. His credits having been made under a system of less money and for products as then valued, would be worth just one-half as much as before; that is to say, they would command just one-half the products of labor. In short, the theory of the

Greenbacker, as thought by the Greenbacker, is a cute device to repudiate about one-half of the value of all debt, contracted prior to his adoption. Of course it is not pretended by any one of this class that the issuance of a few or many greenbacks will have any effect upon the price of gold, or foreign exchange, or that the issuing of greenbacks increases or decreases the sum of wealth, by which wealth should be of less or more price. The effect of the increase of money, as we have seen, is to decrease interest, not increase price. Possibly they get their theories from some of the vagaries of Mr. Mill. The least that can be said of them is, if they want to issue a money which will buy but one-half the product, or, in other words, a depreciated currency, they commit as great a crime as the man who advocates the contraction of the currency. The monometalist wants all the surplus of wealth by his dishonest trick, the Greenbacker wants to repudiate one-half of all obligations by his dishonest trick; that is, taking him according to his own teachings.

NATIONALIZATION OF LAND.

Having had occasion to note the entire fallacy of the theory of Ricardo's law of distribution, and its modern renovation by Mr. George, it might seem superfluous to refer to the remedy proposed by him. I deem it profitable to do so, as I can do no better service than to uproot the subtle fallacy, into which he is led by his idolatry of his interpretation of the law of Ricardo. I am also led to do this, because, while his theory of the cause of poverty is erroneous, his remedy might serve a good purpose. His remedy, I fear, will be found no better than his theory. As before stated, his remedy is a tax upon land, sufficient to confiscate its rental value to the State, in lieu of all other taxes. The reader will bear in mind that Mr. George makes no distinction as to values of land, whether speculative or otherwise. He calls them all rent values.

I never found any statement by Mr. George, as to what the amount of the tax would be, or how it is to be determined what tax will take the value of the land. If we go to political economy, we find it stated there that interest on money determines the value of land. The present tax, which equals the value of land, is, therefore, the money interest on its value. In England it would be from 3 to 4 per cent.; in the State of New York it would be from 5 to 6 per cent.; in Kansas 10 per cent.; in Colorado 15 to 20 per cent.; in China 20 to 30 per cent., and in India 30 to 50 per cent.

Mr. George carefully states that this tax is to be levied upon land values only, excluding all improvements. Take this as a basis in the United States, and what would be the result? The total assessed value of agricultural lands is about ten billions, say three billions is improvements (a small estimate), and this leaves seven billions to tax. This at 6 per cent. would produce $420,000,000; at 7 per cent. $490,000,000 of tax; at 8 per cent. $560,000,000. Now the total tax of the United States in 1880 was a little over $700,000,000. Mr. George would add the value of the land in the cities and towns upon which are business blocks, and would, exclusive of buildings, get possibly two billions more to tax, which, at 8 per cent., would produce just about enough to run the government, National, State, and town and county, as they are now run. It is therefore a grave doubt whether there would be provided under this theory, enough money to pay ordinary public expenses as they now exist, even if all real estate and land values were taxed at average interest on money.

Even though there should thus result sufficient to meet public expenses, what would there have been accomplished? This tax would destroy all speculative rent, or, to follow his theory, you must still raise the tax until it does take away the value of the land. If 8 per cent. will not do this, then it must be raised to 10 per cent. or 20 per cent., or even to 50 per cent. This is the essence of the whole theory—to destroy all motive for investing in land. A tax which will do this, and at the same time cover all expenses of government, is the only tax which will answer the ends of his theory.

The first effect would be to put back in the public domain all land not cultivated or used. No taxes would thereafter, come from such land. This would compel another increase of tax upon the land which continued in use.

2nd. No person could occupy this public domain without paying full interest upon the assessed value thereof.

3rd. No person would voluntarily occupy any land, unless he could make this tax and profit upon his own capital equal to interest.

4th. The very few who could do this, to-wit: a small class of middle men, transporters and manufacturers would charge this, as they now do, as expense upon price of goods, and collect it out of the vast majority of society who work for wages, or work on land with their capital at the margin, or pinch it directly out of wages on account of enforced idleness caused by high interest.

5th. The man without capital would not be able to go on to the public domain, having nothing to cultivate with or secure rent. I therefore conclude that the poor man is better off now than he could be then, for if he had capital to secure rent, he would now have capital to buy the same land, or at least to secure its purchase money. By saving a little for a few years, he could pay back the loan, and own the land forever free from rent. Under Mr. George's system, when he became old and decrepit and unable to pay the rent, the tax gatherer would evict him, confiscate his labor in the land, and leave him a beggar by the wayside. A poor man can go anywhere in the United States, and I think almost any place on earth, except, perhaps, in some portions of Ireland, and do better than to adopt Mr. George's theory.   He can rent lands already improved and in cultivation for less than the money interest upon assessed value of land and improvement. This plan would defeat the very object for which it was intended.   It shuts the poor man out from the land, and places the burden of society upon those least able to bear the burden of taxation.

The inherent and subtle fallacy of this theory, and that which gives it a show of plausibility, is that it constantly confounds land values, with rent values. Taking rent by taxation is appropriating natural opportunities. Taking the increase caused by the growth of society is taking what is styled the "unearned increment" given to the individual by the labor of others. But as I have shown no rent accrues in the increased price of capitalized land (land used exclusively to place and employ capital upon), and hence a tax upon this value is not the appropriation of rent, but an appropriation of a part of the increment of money and capital. This increment (profit and interest) is just as much an "unearned increment" as rent, and originates wholly from the increase of society. Now, Mr. George proposes to continue in full force the present system, by which, I have shown, the whole increase of society as a sequence of law is absorbed by a few and tax out of them a small portion of this "unearned increment," viz.: The proportion invested in land, to the whole value of the total investment—land and capital erected and operated thereon. Now, whatever may be said of the propriety of absorbing this increment of money and capital, the monstrous injustice and folly of this mode of attempting to acomplish this object is apparent. Nowhere is there any uniformity of relation of land to the capital erected or operated thereon. Upon land side by side, of the same value may be capital of ten or twenty times the amount respectively; the one absorbing of this "unearned increment" ten or one hundred fold, while the tax would be exactly equal. The tax of the one would be ten or an hundred times greater than the other relatively. If this increase is the property of society and is to be confiscated by society, justice demands it should all be taken, or taken proportionately.

But this is not the worst feature of the case. Such a tax would not fall upon this land or capital or money at all. It would be charged upon the products of the manufacturer, placed upon the price of goods of the middleman, added to discounts, taken out of the tenant, and passed over upon the laborer and producer at the margin just as it now is.

So long as society regulates its money so that the necessities of the bulk of producers makes them constantly compete for credit, money and voluntarily stored capital will shirk all the burdens of taxation. They will coerce out of production whatever they pay by adding to profit and interest.

When Mr. George thus substitutes profit and interest for rent (probably by mistake), he not only abandons the whole theory upon which his explanation of poverty rests, but actually pro-poses a remedy which perpetuates the present iniquitious system of distribution, and which, in results, can do nothing but aggravate and inten-sify the evil consequences which flow there-from.

It is objectionable on other grounds; all strong, just and progressive governments are based upon the independence and manhood of its members. No manhood or independence can be maintained unless man are rooted to the soil. The reliance for a home, or a livelihood, upon the change of government officials, change in the judgments of men, the growth of society, the increase of ap-praisements without the increase of producing capacity, change of seasons, of sickness and mis-fortune, which would make a home a football of circumstances, would destroy all independence or motive of independence. Land sufficient to the support of parents, and offspring to maturity, safe against all claims except the support of the state, is the sure basis of independent acting and voting.

So again this system would produce a surface, straggling, exhaustive culture Under such circumstances the capitalist would use his resources to exhaust the land, and make all the present return, with a view of letting it go back to the state. One would scarcely plant a vineyard, or build a permanent house, when he knew that he or his own, might not possess them. Would any one voluntarily build houses or business blocks upon land where the rent was liable to double or treble as the years slipped by? Men do this on leases or on perpetual rent, but men are apt to run shy of rack-rent, even if levied for the benevolent purpose of saving a large class of citizens from taxes more equitable than their own.

But the system is unjust as well as impracticable. All the agricultural land upon the face of the globe, which have been used for one hundred years (and I think for fifty), has, at the average rate of interest, been paid for to society from one to twenty times the value of its present appraisement. Take a piece of land open to entry in Kansas thirty years ago. The purchaser then surrendered to the state $1.25 per

acre or $200 per quarter section.   He has since
paid taxes on this land at an average valuation
of $600 per quarter at least, and at the rate of 1
per cent. taxes.   One per cent. on $600 is 3 per
cent. on $200.   The average of interest has been
at least 10 per cent. per annum.   So he has paid
at the rate of 13 per cent. on $200 for thirty
years.   Money at 13 per cent. doubles in five
and one-half years compounded.   So the land
cost, or the state or society has received for the
surrender of its right to this land in 1861, $400;
1867, $800; 1873, $1600; in 1878, $3,200; 1885,
$6,400, and in 1889 it will amount to $12,800.
There are very few quarter sections of land in
the state of half this value.   The Island of Man-
hattan, on which is built the city of New York,
cost in 1621 the sum of $25, which at compound
interest exceeds all the present value of the
land, all it ever produced and all improvements
upon the island to-day, estimated at from one to
two billions of dollars.   It is no answer that
society has not had this value out of this particular land.   That is not the lookout of the
purchaser.   The state has had this money, and
could by loaning it have had the accumulation
by waiting and receiving the interest.   The in-
indestructible and original powers of the land

were exchanged for a power to gather more wealth than the net return from the land; society has had it; if society had paid it out for guns and wars and other needs, so much the worse for society. It has parted with its right to the land for an equivalent and more than a just compensation, and the power does not exist in society to annul its own contracts or confiscate the land, so long as the balance of community are deprived of no rights thereby.

At the risk of repeating, I must beg every one to bear in mind, what most writers constantly forget, and Mr. George occasionally with the rest, that rent is not what is paid for, or does it arise out of the improvement upon land. The price paid for a dwelling house, the use of a store house, are not rent; they are payment for capital. The payment for an improved farm in part, a small part, for rent, and a large part for the use of improvements (capital). This total payment is so high, because cost of capital is so high, and capital commands so much, because it can be turned into money, and produce interest, or, if stored with loaned money, it must bring interest or lose. Labor pinched out, comes in constant competition with labor, and wages fall, and hence land rises. How would a man demand rent, if

labor commanded all the product, except the
small portion which would store capital? The
owner would be out the use of his land, improvements, taxes, and wear and tear. The value of
land depends upon how cheap labor is, not labor
upon the price of land. Land is valueless without labor. Reduce transportation to a minimum,
profit to 3 per cent., and interest likewise, and
you would at once reduce rental profits in New
York City. Railroads would be built out, and
cars running every three minutes to towns scat-
tered all about the city, with nominal fare, where
would be cheap dwellings to hire, because capital would be cheap, and cost for use propor-
tioned. Hundreds of millions of dollars which
are now exacted for the use of wind, would stay
in Western and Southern States. Shoe factories,
woolen factories, cotten factories, would be built
there which are pinched out now by high interest. The relative productiveness of land would
become equalized, and economic rent would
cease altogether.

Mr. George's theory is contrary to natural
justice. The right to individual ownership of
anything, Mr. George asserts, is derived from
the right to personal liberty. From the personal
right to myself and my acts, arises the right to

my labor and fruits. Under this theory strictly construed, there is no personal right to anything. Nothing on earth was created by labor. The pen I write with, is not the product of labor, as Mr. George affirms. The material was the product of the occult forces of nature. These forces combine the oxygen and carbon, and produced the iron contained in it. Man stole the material from nature, adds a little of his labor and calls it his own. It is his, society consenting, and it not interferring with the rights of others. The same right exists to any portion of nature or its products. The ground I took and cleared, and plowed, and seeded, and made worth all it is worth. My labor reduced it, and brought it from a worthless waste to supply the necessities of many. I own it because my labor is incorporated in it, my capital fertilized it, because it is for the public good, society consenting.

The system of land holding in Europe, by which a certain class, known as peasant proprietors, are attached to the soil, is much more in accord with the theory of Mr. George, and a much better solution of the land question than tax system advanced by him. These holdings, established ceturies ago, are on a basis of a perpetual rent, established then. These holdings have

been demonstrated to be in accordance with the
rent theory of Mr. George.   Rent, or the natural
powers of land, never increases.   It rather decreases, unless constantly recuperated by labor,
and added sustenance.   The multiplication of the
power of production, has more than kept pace
with the demand for products, and hence, rent
has never risen on the whole, and probably never will.   The evidence of the rise of rent, says
Mr. Ricardo, is the increased pressure of population against land, causing a rise in price.   This
has not occurred.   What Mr. George and Mr.
Mill take for the evidence of the rise of rent, is
the pressure of interest and profit against production.   It is this which absorbs production, as
is evidenced by fact everywhere.

If this remedy of Mr. George was put in operation the only effect would be to drive from the field,
all voluntary producers of raw products.   The burdens of society would be added to their now too
heavy burdens, would drive this class of laborers,
who now work at the very margin of wages and
profit, utterly to the wall, while those who now
have all the surplus of production, would have,
with less effort, the surplus of all society's earnings.   This idea of "free land" is really the one
which catches the attention of all the men who

fall a prey to the doctrine of Henry George. Without reading the work or understanding his remedy, they think he means to give them free land. Free land with a rent, which could be increased and must be increased constantly to keep up the expenses of government, would be a very inviting freedom in actual experience. With a free profit, free interest, free to be made what some particular class see fit to make them, the producer of raw products would be driven to the condition of the Irish serf, and the manufacturer and transporter to the condition of absentee landlords.

His theory of poverty, and his theory of remedy, neither of them touch the trouble in society. If he should change his remedy, so that land held by the individuals, as private property, but not occupied or used for productive purposes, should be taxed at the rate of interest on money, and that all land used or cultivated should be entirely free from taxation, then indeed would Mr. George confer a boon upon those whom he seeks to assist. This would drive all land out of the hands of speculators into the hands of the State; would leave all such land a free common, and encourage the pursuit of labor upon land, from which originally comes all wealth, and place the burdens upon those best able to bear the same. Though this would be in a greater measure just, and make an approach to a relief of poverty, being really of some service to labor, yet like all the remedies before suggested it is but paliative. The real trouble then as now, would be that the laborer would not get the product of his toil.

As long as the average of interest is above the average increase of wealth, there is no voluntary motive to store wealth below this interest. And enough wealth would be absorbed out of wealth, produced by capital stored below this interest from necessity, to pay the higher interest and profit on money and capital stored thereby.

This is unalterable.

The coming fate is no more certain than the operation of this law.

Turn it or distort it as we may, high interest and profit are paid by somebody. The average of production pays them; so that any man who goes on to free land, and makes on his capital 3 per cent., which is the very outside (as table iii., appendix, shows), all this would go to pay somebody's 6 per cent. profit and interest, and he would work for bare wages, his land and capital bringing nothing, though in reality above the margin of cultivation.

And so I am driven to the conclusion, evident from the first, that as the true condition of society was veiled from the mind of all writers, so it is an impossibility for any one of them, with the clouds hanging over their vision, to ever conceive of an intelligent remedy.

The remedy must be broader and more comprehensive, must embrace all the complex relations of society, from the beginning of production to the end of distribution; must comprehend the inate differences everywhere existing in men, their powers, capacities, opportunities, strength and weakness, diversity of likes and dislikes, establish justice upon the throne of society, and secure the members thereof perfect liberty without trammel or hindrance, each for himself to run his own race to success or defeat.

The remedies suggest themselves:

1st. The cause of unjust accumulation of wealth, and extreme poverty, are primarily caused by the contraction of money.

2nd. By laws creating a violation of the natural law of acquisition of land.

3rd. By granting special privileges to corporations.

To correct the first:

Make a system of money to conform to justice, so that the average of interest shall average with the increase of wealth.

2nd. Prohibit all estates in land for more than life, or lives in being; and, make it free to sale and exchange like other property.

3rd. Should the natural law of competition thus established be insufficient to curb created monopolies, let the government use public credit to compete with them or own and use them on the basis of average profit.

The first of these remedies is radical and indispensible; without it poverty and unequal conditions are a necessity.

I believe all others would follow as a necessary sequence of this. I believe that the stimulous thus given to labor and capacity to supply itself with opportunities, would so act upon distribution that land would be worthless to any person, except the producer himself. Under such circumstances, no man would be compelled to work for another man. He would work for himself if he chose. Lest this be a mistake, I include the other remedies as a present, possible, necessary, paliative means of producing equality, and it now only remains to ascertain—can money be made to conform to justice? How? Or by what means?

MONEY.

CHAPTER II.

WHAT IS MONEY?

The essential character and functions of money. Its origin and features which distinguish it from every other thing in society.

One of the principal troubles in the promulgation or acquisition of truth, is the fact that the human mind, in all its operations, is automatic.

The amount of knowledge of every individual is the result of first or transmitted impressions; or, in other words, of education. Impressions are engraved upon the memory, like the impression of a stamp upon wax, and stay so fixed, unless reflection remove them, or other impressions take their place. A child first learns the multiplication table, by repeating over and over again, without reason or comprehension—six times six are thirty-six. Association gradually fixes this succession of ideas, and ever afterward, with or without reason, six times six is thirty-six. So of any theory, scientific or practical. What has been read or been taught becomes fixed and fossilized in the mind, and whether true or false, it is ever afterward utterly impossible to eradicate the impressions thus made. To teach any new doctrine is like teaching in an unknown tongue. Every man has written upon the black-board of his mind some such thing as the following:

"Gold is a standard of value."

"Silver is a standard of value."

"Gold and silver are money."

And although there may not be a respectable economist who endorses such a sentiment, yet if I, or anyone, should presume to question these impressions, the natural ego, the man himself, this bundle of impressions, which has been forming since childhood, either turns himself away with a sneer, or fights against the truth, no matter how very true it is, or how much he may be interested in its being true. So most reformers are compelled to await the growth of a new generation of black-boards, upon which are written :

"All men are born free and equal."

"Slavery is a crime against humanity."

And so it may possibly be that it will take a generation to effectually write upon the consciences of man :

"Interest above the average of increase of wealth is a crime not second to slavery."

"A government which maintains such interest 'is a covenant with hell, etc.'"

"Freedom and such injustice cannot remain long under one government."

And yet I am constrained by the mighty weight of conviction which bears down upon me, to believe that these sentiments will be written there, and written there speedily, or all free government, founded, as they are, upon no pretense of justice, will pass away and give place to governments of force. Men have no affection for a government when injustice is stamped upon its laws. The freedom to work for a privileged few is no great blessing. Starvation under a monarchy is just as sweet as under a republic.

I make these remarks in order to impress upon any seeker after truth two facts :

1st. The necessity of laying aside for the time being, the previous education he has received as to the character and manner of making money.

2nd. The necessity of constantly bearing in mind, that it is almost an impossibility to get out of any work extant a single correct idea of money. They do almost invariably confound money with wealth, money with gold and silver, interest with profit. When they mean one thing they speak of the other, and vice versa, and every statement where they use them interchangably must of necessity be wrong. Whenever I find Mr. Mill, or Smith, or Ricardo, speaking of money, as money, they often tell the truth; when of money, as gold or silver, they never tell the truth. All gold is not money, all money not gold. Gold used as capital is governed by the law of capital. Gold used as money ceases to be capital or wealth, or a commodity, and is not governed by the laws of capital or wealth, but by the laws of money.

Having thus cautioned every one to keep a weather eye out, I quote Adam Smith as good authority on money, when he says:

Book ii., chapter i. "When by any particular sum of money we mean not only to express the amount of metal

pieces of which it is composed, but to include in its sig-
nification some obscure reference to the goods which can
be had in exchange for them; the wealth or revenue
which it in this case denotes is equal only to one of the
two values, which are thus intimated somewhat ambigu-
ously by the same words, and to the latter, more properly
than to the former, to the money's worth more properly
than to the money. Thus, if a guinea be the weekly
pension of a particular person, he can, in the course of
the week, purchase with it a certain quantity of subsistence, convenience and amusements. In proportion
as this quantity is great or small, so are his real riches
his real weekly revenues. His weekly revenue is not
certainly equal to the guinea, and to what can be purchased with it, but only to the one or other of these two
equal values, and to the latter more properly than to the
former to the guinea's worth rather than to the guinea.
If the pension of such a person was paid to him, not in
gold, but in a weekly bill for a guinea, his revenue would
not so properly consist in the pieces as in what could be
got for it. A guinea may be considered as a bill for a
certain quantity of necessities and convenience upon all
the tradesmen in the neighborhood. The revenue of the
person to whom it is paid does not so properly consist of
the pieces of gold as in what he can get for it, or in what
he can exchange it for. If it could be exchanged for
nothing it would, like a bill upon a bankrupt, be of no
more value than the most useless piece of paper."

Thus, Mr. Adam Smith distinctly emphasizes
what I say, that we are apt to confound the
credit which is in the money to the pieces of
gold which carry the credit; or, in other words,

this definition is that (a guinea) money is an order on society, drawn and authenticated and guaranteed to be what its face represents, and made to represent credit (all future payments) by being made legal tender. That money is a function, its positive object being distribution, with its concurrent and resultant effects in society heretofore described.

Mr. Mill, speaking of the essential character of money, chapter vii., section 3, book iii., says:

"It must be evident, however, that the mere introduction of a particular mode of exchanging things for one another, by first exchanging a thing for money and then exchanging the money for something else, makes no difference in the essential character of the transaction. It is not with money that things are really purchased. Nobody's income (except that of the gold or silver miner) is derived from the precious metals. The pounds or shillings that a person receives weekly or yearly are not what constitute his income. They are a sort of ticket or order, which he can present for payment at any shop he pleases, and which entitle him to receive a certain value of any commodity that he makes choice of. The farmer pays his laborers and his landlord in these tickets as the most convenient plan for him and them; but their real income is his corn, cattle and hay, and it makes no difference whether he distributes it to them directly or sells it for them and gives them the price. * * It is a machine for doing quickly and commodiously what would be done, though less quickly and commodiously, without it."

Thus, Mr. Mill says here that money is a means to an end; "a machine" and its function is what he long ago told us—"the precise function of money is to distribute." This is one of the few places in Mr. Mill's work on political economy where he speaks of money. On almost all occasions he has gold or commodity value or influence mixed up with money value, and there is scarcely a statement upon this subject made by him, which is not vitiated by ambiguity. I shall have occasion to call particular attention to these hereafter.

Mr. Ricardo says:

"Productions are always bought by productions or by services; money is only the medium by which the exchange is effected."

He always, however, confounds gold with money, and more than any man living or dead is responsible for the total want of appreciation of money in production.

Mr. Bastiat says, chapter xxi., translated by David A. Wells:

"You have a dollar. What does it imply in your hand? It is, as it were, the witness, and proof that you have, at some time or other performed some labor which instead of turning to your advantage, you have bestowed upon society as represented by the person of your client (employer or debtor). This coin testifies that you have performed a service for society, and moreover it shows the

value of it. It bears witness besides that you have not
yet obtained from society a real equivalent service to
which you have a right. To place you in a condition to
exercise this right, at the time and in the manner you
please, society as represented by your client has given you
an acknowledgement, a title to a dollars worth of property, which only differs from executive title, by bearing
its value in itself, and if you are able to read with you
minds eye, the inscription stamped upon it, you will distinctly decipher these words: "Pay the bearer a service
equivalent to what he has rendered to society, the value
received being shown proved and measured by that which
is represented by me."

Thus Mr. Bastiat fully recognizes the fact that
money is not wealth.   That the gold pieces, and
the silver pieces, and the paper pieces are only
instruments of credit; an invention, and creation
of society to effect distribution.   And notwith-
standing Mr. Bastiat sees this, that the gold is
not the payment, that the gold pieces or silver
pieces are for the time being but a check, a
counter, just the same as a theatre ticket, or a
ticket at a lunch counter, or in other words that
money is a public credit given to paper or gold
or silver by the decree of the State, so as to
represent its face value, yet in ten lines, or at
least in ten pages, he will confound money with
bullion, its functions with its material, and go off
into just such vagaries as all metalists or mono-

metalists.   The logic of consequences which flow from these definitions are :

1st.   Money being the function given to matter, to carry value, and represent public credit, it can only be conferred by society through law.

2nd.   That any material which can be made to represent a fixed value, can be made money.

3d.   That up to the public credit, it can be increased or diminished as society chooses, to accomplish the best interests of society.

4th.   That it can be made to represent any value desired, or established as a standard of payment.

CHAPTER III.

By Whom Made.

Essentially an exercise of sovereignty, and its
 powers confined to the jurisdiction which
 originates it.

Money not being a creation of labor or a
natural product, but an invention or construction,
its functions and powers are confined to the
jurisdiction in which it originates.   Laws of all
nations differ as to this, as in all other matters.
There is no law or comity of nations, in regard
to money.   No two nations agree as to what
shall or shall not be money; or how much they
shall have, each satisfying themselves, by acting
without any judgment, or system or understanding. Thus, about seven-tenths of the world adopt
as a standard of payment, some form or subdi-
vision of silver, and make their payments corres-

pond to the price of the subdivisions of this metal. About one-fifth of the world use gold and silver in some ratio (from 15 to 16 of silver to 1 of gold), as a standard of payment, and about one-twentieth of the world adopt gold as the single standard of payment. All these have auxiliary debased coins, which by law are made conformable to the gold and silver coins in payment, and almost all civilized nations, so called, have paper auxiliary money, which, redeemable or irredeemable in the gold or silver coins, is, by operation of law, made to represent the price of the standard of payments. These coins and auxiliary paper, by operation of law in each government, become the representatives of credit, and all contracts and credits are liquidated, and put at an end, by passing these from hand to hand. The folly, therefore, of talking, as most political writers do, of gold and silver, as a synonym of money, or of using such expressions as "money of the world," is made apparent. Also, the folly of continuing the illusion which most economists like to do, that money is a refined mode of barter; for were this the case (I desire this to be noticed) when the government had determined what should be the material, fineness,

and amount of the same to be used in coin, and
had proceeded to subdivide, coin and authenticate
their amount and fineness, this would end the interference of government in business.   Each individual would then put such prices upon them
as he chose, receive them or not receive them, in
liquidating a contract.   Such stuff would not be
money.   Half the mistakes of political economists are made in trying to class and reason
about such coins as money.   The essential
power of the nation to make these subdivisions
represent a particular price and liquidate contracts, must be added or it is not money.   This
is a national power, ends with the jurisdiction of
the State. The moment, therefore, gold or silver
coins or money go out of the jurisdiction which
originated them, they cease to be money, and are
sold by weight as bullion, or are received according to the value which may be legally given
them, in any country where they may be found.

This power given by the State is the source of
the fearful significance of money in society. This
legal function to represent all exchanges, all exertion, all labor, all credit, or future payments, is
just as important and essential to the existence
of society as any other function of sovereignty.
A population of ten to the square mile could

scarce survive without some form of money. It is as innate as the power to create a court of justice or establish an army. It is just as absurd and criminal an exercise of this prerogative of government to allow an individual to interfere with the issue of money, to expand or contract its volume, as it would be to allow an individual to constitute himself a tax collector, levy taxes, determine amount, collect the same and pay them out as he saw fit. And when political economists, as they frequently do, assert that it is of little moment how much or how little of money is established in a nation, they are talking of the simple, or primitive, or barter use of money. This simple use of money can in most cases be accomplished by the use of private credit as well as by the use of money itself, but when we are compelled to go beyond the slow accumulation and savings of capital, and utilize the forces of nature to the uttermost, this simple and purile notion of money must be discarded and the functions and powers recognized which underlie all great progress in society. The power inheres in government, and is essential to its existence to confer this function upon money than which, there is no one of greater moment to the interests of humanity, which, though felt by

all historians and thinking men, has always been
obscured, if not wholly hid, by the ambiguities
by which political economists have surrounded
it from Adam Smith to Mill and Bastiat.

CHAPTER IV.

MONEY

Made out of anything which can be made to represent public credit.

As money is not a product of labor, not growing, not fashioned, or made in the sense of making physical things, as it does not labor, but is simply a function given to material things to convey value, it must be self-evident that it can be made out of anything which will perform the function, *i. e.*, convey the value of the standard adopted as payment. In early times, when governments were neither honest or stable, and there was, therefore, very little credit, gold and silver were used as the best means of cheap barter. As soon as society advanced, so credits were made, and men made contracts for

future payments, gold and silver were naturally
adopted by most nations as the standard of payment.   History shows that almost every article
has been adopted by nations for this purpose,
but most frequently the precious metals ; not, as
is commonly supposed, because they are a
" standard of value," but for various reasons,
among which are :

1st.   Their average cost runs nearer an average equation of equality with all other products
than any other two products of man's labor—or,
to state it possibly more clearly, they cost nearer
an average amount of labor, interest and profit
than other products of industry.

2nd.   Because they resist the erosion of almost all acids.

3rd.   Because they are easily subdivided.

4th.   Because there is considerable labor used
in producing a small quantity.

Now, for the above and for one other reason,
which I find recorded nowhere in political writings, I admit that gold and silver are the best
standards for payment, but that they are fit to
be commonly used as money I utterly deny.
This reason is simply as follows: When a nation
has established any metal of a particular fineness
as a standard of payment, and made it freely

coined at the mint, the coins at that time represent the value of the bullion practically (seniorage
slightly changes this).   Now, this money, when
so constituted, becomes the public estimate, to
which all values are referred. Should there be any
change in quantity, in supply or demand of other
products, it is at once felt or is reflected in price.
Should bullion become more plenty, *i e.*, gold
and silver and a consequent decline in price of
these metals commence to occur, there is a perpetual demand, a place where it can be absorbed,
a ready sale at the mint, and then it ceases to
be bullion and ceases to bear prices. If bullion gets scarce and there is danger of a rise
in price, the coins will be smelted into bullion,
and thus bring the price of bullion down.

In other words, the making money out
of a metal, of which there is so little, that
there will always be a demand for all or
more than there is for sale, will keep the price of
bullion up to the price of money; and the fact
that there is always a supply of coin, which can
be made into bullion, will keep bullion down to
the price of money. For this reason, far more
than from the fact of its even cost of production,
money holds bullion to the price you start with.
A little reflection will show that, were it not for

this, bullion would change in price like other commodities, for it is a product of about 33 per cent. profit and interest and 66 per cent. wages. Now, the profit and interest in supplies and transportation, which are figured into bullion, change about as much, and are figured in as often as in any business except manufacturing, and these changes and fluctuations would impress themselves upon the metal and produce a variation of price, were there not a flux into which it could flow and be lost. But with this balance wheel, coinage, I agree with Ricardo that gold and silver are the best and nearest standard to determine the price of payment, but, as I said before, are unfit for use as money:

1st.   Because of weight; in transportation and handling their exclusive use would cost from one-eighth to one-half per cent. more than certificates.

2nd.   Because they are not easily concealed. Insurance against risk render them from one-eighth to one-quarter per cent. less value than paper.   A man can carry $20,000 to $100,000 of paper money and no one be the wiser; $1,000 in silver weighs sixty pounds; $5,000 in gold is a load too heavy for any man to carry any length of time.

3rd. Abrasion of coin constantly used destroys about one-quarter per cent. per annum,
which is an absolute loss of valuable material.

4th. But the real reason why gold and silver
are unfit for money, is for the same reason that
they are so good a standard for payment; that
is, they are liable to be coined and uncoined.
They, as bullion, are capital and in demand as
capital the world over; this causes them to
shift from one country to another, not as demanded for money, but more often just opposite
to the demand and want of money. Now, as I
have shown a steady, stable, increasing volume
of money, is the most important element in a
progressive nation. When, from any commodity
demand, gold flows out of a country which uses
it exclusively as a means of circulating its credit,
the effect is to contract such credit, leaving behind business panics and depressions. In the
country where it goes, it may be consumed as
capital, or it may increase the money volume.
If the latter, capital will be stored rapidly and
business activity prevail. Any change in supply
or demand of commodities may send it back
again, leaving behind a like destruction of credit.
Thus. as it goes from one to the other it produces alternate business exaltation and heart-

rending despair. It would be amusing, were it not so sad a picture in the back ground, to read our own gifted Carey, as he lauds gold and silver to the skies, calling them the God-given blessings to mankind; the very means of association, as he calls money, and they as a synonym. All the time he seems to be utterly oblivious that the gold and silver which comes into a country and is made into money, and seems, as it stimulates business, to be so great a blessing, just left some other country, and is liable any day to leave this with ruined homes, sorrow, devastation and tears. I am constrained of the idea that gold and silver are good for to believe, as I see the extent of the influence money, "the only money," "real money" and the work of devastation wrought, of hopes blasted, of nations destroyed, fortunes swept into the abyss of ruin, asylums filled with lunatics and poorhouses with paupers, of theft and murder and arson, of the helpless struggle of one half of mankind since the dawn of civilization, the benumbing of every faculty which exalts man above a beast of burden, the stunning of every aspiration which lifts from degradation, all of which may be traced to such ideas; that if the arch fiend of the pit had been called upon to congregate, the most abject and cunning of all his hosts, who had been engaged since eternity in fomenting schemes of woe and torture, and in solemn conclave demanded of them to devise a scheme, which in itself should concentrate the heights and depths of bitterness and woe for mankind, there would, without a moment's hesitation, have gone up from the lowest dungeon depths to the highest wall and battlement one wild refrain, "make gold and silver the only money."

Coin gold and silver freely at price as is best for the nation, so by the influx of coinage the price can be made to remain comparatively stationary, and then make money out of paper, money fit for civilization, which shall carry this value.

CHAPTER V.

QUANTITY OF MONEY.

Can be made in any quantity and maintain its representative value so long as average interest is not below average increase of profit. Errors growing out of confounding gold and silver, with money, corrected.

From what I have already written it would seem to be self-evident that money can be made to comply with the demands of justice. It is the exact and necessary conclusion which can alone be drawn from all definitions of money by economists. Nevertheless, Mr. John Stuart Mill and Mr. Bastiat (and most all modern leaders of thought follow them) assert distinctly that money is a commodity; that gold and silver are money; that the terms are synonymous; that they are governed by the same laws, etc., etc.

Now, I do not wish to leave behind me one single vestage of this sophism, and hence will quote Mr. Mill's statement, and thus prevent any misapprehension or misunderstanding. Book iii., chapter viii., section 3, he says:

"Money is a commodity and its value is determined like that of other commodities." * * * Chapter viii., section 2. "The value of purchasing power of money depends in the first instance on demand and supply. * * * The supply of commodities means the quantity offered for sale. * * * In point of fact, money is bought and sold like other things when other things are bought and sold for money. * * *

"Section 4. The propositions we have laid down respecting the quantity of money in circulation must be understood as applying only to a state of things in which money, that is gold and silver, is the exclusive instrument of exchange, and actually passes from hand to hand at every purchase, credit in any shape being unknown. * * * That an increase of the quantity of money raises prices, and a diminution lowers them, is the most elementary proposition in the theory of currency."

These quotations embody the sentiment which pervades and perverts every department of education, and utterly incapacitates society from appreciating or utilizing the money function. That the casual reader should be misled by statements made with such apparent confidence and candor, is not so very strange, but that teachers, educators and critics, in the light of facts which he knew and they knew, should be led to sanction such absurdities and contradictions as these quotations necessitate, if read litterly, is a wonder too marvelous for comprehension.

Now, when Mr. John Stuart Mill made such statements he knew at the time that there was gold and silver plate in England, there was jewelry and watches of gold, which were not money, and therefore when he said gold and' silver are money, he knew he was making a statement which was not scientific. Mr. Mill knew, that the Court of King's Bench of England had decided that the statute makes the coins money; that the common law of England had, from time immemorial, decided that damages on contracts, or liquidated damages, must and could only be paid in money, and he knew that gold and silver could not do this. He therefore knew that he was stating a scientific and legal untruth, when he made this statement. He further knew that gold was not money in China, in South America, Japan or India. He knew that silver was not money in England. He knew that, and says in the very next section, just quoted, "that it is not with money that things are really purchased;" that "money is the mere instrument of transfer;" "was a ticket;" "was a machine." He knew that money had been made out of everything, and at the time was made out of copper, gold silver, tin, paper. He knew at the very moment he wrote, that there existed in the British Isle, a money (he says it is money) made out of paper and only paper—non-redeemable, non-exchangeable—absolute money, fiat money, if you choose, created by law, that law called Peel's act. Now what is the meaning of all this jumble of inconsistencies and contradictions? Are we to suppose that Mr. Mill, in a scientific work, proposes to wipe out the records of time, the decisions of courts, and, above all, existing patent facts? Or did Mr. Mill make a slip when he here called gold and silver money?

The simple truth is, he was not talking about money. He was talking about gold and silver—a commodity, the product of labor—and the effect of the increase as to the demand, on price. He says this as plain as he can in the quotation marked section iv. Substitute "gold and silver" for money in all the previous quotations, and they sound rational. The last quotation has no sense or reason as applied to money, or currency, but in an off-shoot of the old ambiguity, confounding gold, the material, with money, the function. Any other interpretation (a literal interpretation) leads to absurdities as follows:

1st "A" goes into the exchange at 10 o'clock, and corn is worth 40 cents per bushel, and wheat 60 cents per bushel. He goes in again at 11 o'clock and corn is selling at 39 cents per bushel, and wheat at 61 cents per bushel. Mr. Mill's proposition is: That corn brought 40 cents an hour ago, and the same corn brought only 39 cents now, and hence 40 cents has gone up one-fortieth. And just the other way with the wheat. The same penny is worth just one-sixtieth less. Therefore, political economy, by John Stuart Mill, "Money is gone up and money has gone down," at one and the same time. Mr. Mill is riding two horses again.

Absurdity No. 2: That the making of more or less gold into money alters the volume of gold the world over, and decreases its price. I have just shown that this coinage raises the price instead of decreasing it, and tends to hold gold and silver steady in value. Authorizing its coinage makes a new use for the metals.

3rd. That the transportation of a quantity of gold or silver from one country to another, and it there being coined into money, would raise the price of all products there.

The only reason it goes at all is to balance exchanges; that is, the products of one coun-

try are purchased in excess of products sent
from the other ; gold and silver fill the gap. Now
if Mr. Mill's theory were true, and the prices of
other commodities rose, they would immediately
be supplied from abroad, and the gold would
slide back where it came from.   If they stay, it
is because commodities do not rise.   Evidently,
therefore, this money does not necessarily have
anything to do with prices.   It may be used by
the man who receives it to pay labor.   He may
hire hands, who were idle before its advent, and
put them onto land or into factories, and they
immediately go to producing their own wages,
and a surplus over, which will go onto the
market and again lower prices, and again bring
over some more gold, which will again do the
same.

   This is precisely the condition that has been
going on in the United States for nine years.
The gold and silver money has more than
doubled in this short space of time, a large
share of it from importations.   Over eight hundred million, of this currency has come into circulation during this period, and instead of having
depreciated, its relative general value as compared with product, is higher (*i. e.* it will purchase more product) than at the beginning of the

expension. The only perceptible effect, has been the most extraordinary increase in production ever recorded in history. The advance in wealth of the United States has always been the marvel of time. With wonderful resources of land and natural opportunities, with a strong, progressive people, wealth grew spontaneous under the hand of industry, but we had a curse; we had a lie written on our portals, *i. e.* "gold and silver are money," and so we toiled, and we gathered a little production together, and we sent our raw products, which has 12 per cent. of labor (see appendix, table vi.), over to foreign countries, where they had established manufactures, and we brought them back, with 35 to 40 per cent. of interest and profit added, and the 40 per cent. profit took all our raw product and left us in debt, and this balance of debt we were compelled to pay in gold and silver, and as they were our only means of circulating our credit, when they were gone there were no means of liquidating debts, and a panic ensued. Under this disadvantage, our wealth during this period advanced from 1 to 1 ¼ per cent. per annum. The necessities of the war compelled the American people to abandon this false and fraudulent theory of money, and the force of a growing education

on the subject of money drove the rulers in
America to abandon the suicidal policy which
gave the country into the hands of foreign money-
changers (or rather men who loan us wind, and
charge us high interest); we locked the door
on this uneven competition, in which we, with
interest at 6 and 7 per cent., are compelled to
work against competing capital at 2 and 3 per
cent., and the result is, that money has doubled,
all products have, on the average, decreased in
price, and our wealth has advanced, according to
the sworn statement of appraisers, at $3\frac{1}{8}$ per
cent. per annum, and more than this by the estimate of men well posted in such matters. Never
were such results realized before in the world's
history. If we have the wisdom to go on and
increase the quantity of money until interest
drops to meet the rising tide of production, no
human mind can foretell the height of grandeur
and happiness which is in store for the republic.
If we fail to see this, no tongue can depict the
depths to which she will plunge.

4th. That a commodity which has a perpetual demand for its use at a perpetual price, should
change materially in price, is too absurd to argue.

5th. That when there is not enough gold or
silver to supply one-quarter, or at best one-half,

the demand for money at a perpetual price, a little or a greater quantity coming into a country should raise or decrease its price.

6th.   The patent, ever present fact, reluctantly conceded by Mr. Mill, but plainly stated by Mr. Adam Smith, and known of all men everywhere, that the use of money in simply exchanges is not the only or the most common use of money, but that everywhere, in every nation on earth, since money was invented, or used, there has been, is now and ever will be a constant, press- ing, earnest competitive demand, for money for other purposes than barter, for money to loan and to store capital, and when any one can go into the market with this same money, paper, gold or silver, in any country in Europe and sell futures on it, *i. e.*, sell the same money to be de- livered back at the end of one year or six months at an increase double what can be had by the use of average capital in any such nation, any one can see the climax of absurdity of say- ing the quantity of money will cause it to de- preciate, as says Mr. Mill, or that it will flow out, leaving just enough for barter, as says Mr. Smith. There is a perpetual demand for more money for this purpose than has ever been cre- ated.

If fifty or one hundred millions of money could be injected into the circulation of the United States, instead of depreciating its price, 20,000 or 30,000 men would go to work who now work but part of the time. The whole sum would be absorbed in new production com- menced, or in handling production already completed, and by the time this was fairly absorbed more would be needed. This has been done in the United States, every year, but one, for nine years. No nation of modern times has approached the capacity to produce, because they have not realized the importance of this influence of money. The recuperation of nations after great wars or conflagrations demonstrates that there is an inert force, never called out in society, which could and would push the wheels of progress beyond the capacity of ordinary conception, were this not checked.

The better theory and true theory is fast gaining ground that money, as money, has nothing to do with making prices, as Mr. Mill says in the quotation on the nature of money. As money, it is simply the equation of relation between commodities—carries or represents value almost unchangeable, being about the same in cost of production.

But the most satisfactory proofs of all theories are facts. Tested by these, it is almost enough to make an angel weep for humanity, when we read these theories of economists in the light of every day occurrences.

France has three times as much money as the United States, twice as much as Great Britain in proportion to population. If Mr. Mill's theory had any truth in it, an ounce of good gold would be worth three times as much in the United States as in France, and twice as much as in Great Britain, and products would be vice versa. We draw a veil over the bantling of "gold money," "commodity money," and rear an altar to its memory with an inscription on it: "Died young.' "Died of too much cold fact."

And in our sorrow go back to our demonstration and the authority of Adam Smith, which shows that the increase of money necessarily decreases the price of all products in which interest and profit enter, and only raises the price of raw products by an increased production, increased demand and increased wages; and affirm, without a doubt or hesitation or fear, that money can be created enough to answer the ends of justice.

How much? There is no light upon this sub-

ject in the history of the world. As no nation
ever attempted to solve the mystery, it is a mystery to-day. What should be the rule is to supply a quantity of money sufficient to meet the
wants of trade, and have enough over to loan, to
bring interest down to the average increase of
wealth. If, by any careful process of computation, it was found to be 3 or 4 per cent. gradually
infused into the circulation, money enough to
reduce interest to this amount, or make an automatic arrangement so money could be had at
this per cent.

Samples are around us. France has $50.00
per capita of money composed of gold, silver and
paper. She has her interest very low, from 3 to
3½ per cent. for good mercantile paper. I am
not informed as to the rate of her increase of
wealth. But I know that within an area of about
three-fourths the State of Texas, a portion of
which, by ancient land usages, is kept from the
free use, according to the ordinary laws of competition, she subsists a population of nearly forty
millions of people. She is surrounded by war-
like monarchies, who compel her to expend
enormous sums upon a standing army and navy,
to keep out of productive employment a half
million of her most able bodied producers; to

pay interest on a debt four times as large as that
of the United States; yet her people live and
prosper, and there is not a great deal to boast of
in wealth, prosperity and wages between the two
republics.   Put all the population of the United
States on a proportionate area of land, say upon
the land of Pennsylvania, Ohio, Illinois, Indiana
and Iowa, leave the interest on money as it is,
and give them the additional burdens that France
has, and the government would last probably
two months.

I do not say $50 or $40 per capita; I simply
say, make enough to conform to justice; and I
further say, that any constitution which does not
provide for the issuing of money enough to keep
interest down to the average increase of wealth,
in the language of Wendall Phillips, is:

" A league with hell and a covenant with the
devil."

And I am far more justified in saying this,
than of a constitution upholding African slavery.
That was only the debasement and robbery of
the labor of a class ; this is the robbery of the
human race.   Worse yet ; it bars them from the
use of their labor, from opportunities provided
by Providence, and compels them to stand idly
by and witness the aged mother and helpless

babe wither and pine from hunger and want of bread, which this very government gives, by this very mode, to some glutton or debauche.

CHAPTER VI.

How to Give Par Value.

Rules which should govern the issue of money.

It is not the intention of this work to enter into the particulars of the details of government, or to enlarge upon particular modes of accomplishing results. My desire will be accomplished, if I impress upon the mind of the reader, in the shortest way possible, the facts which underlie the progress of the race, so that they may be understood and appreciated.

In this age of progress, we are fast learning that the wellfare of man cannot be pinned to the dictum of any theorist. One by one of past idols are being shattered by newly-born facts, and proofs furnished that men are but men. The car of progress waits upon no man. If he puts his punny individuality before the wellfare of many, it will grind him to powder. Representative men in every generation present the most advanced thoughts of their day, but it is seldom unclouded by their own personality, or the prejudices or necessities of their nationality. Mr. Smith, in his exposition of the errors of the Mercantile system, undoubtedly demonstrated that gold and silver are not objects of commerce, and he was, therefore, supposed to have demonstrated that money was of no account, and that only so much money would stay in any country as could be used under a system of barter; that as a broad, scientific fact, free trade among nations was the true interest of all men.

Solid fact has so altered all these theories, that their author would not recognize his progeny. They have shown and demonstrated, that so far as gold and silver are concerned they are of little moment to humanity; that were they both thrown into the crater of Vesuvius, the world need not stop or be impeded in its onward march, but they have also demonstrated that after a certain stage of development, money is absolutely indispensible to the progress of a race.

Has demonstrated that free trade may or may not be for the best interests of man.

That what is good for one nation is seldom good for another, or her people; that the good, or rather the upbuilding of some nations and their institutions, is not for the good of humanity; that free trade is always an arbitrary question, and always more or less directly and arbitrarily dependent upon the question of money.

That any nation which so regulates its money as to have an advantage of 1 per cent. interest, other things being equal, can break down all the industries of any other country laboring under this disadvantage; that this interest is purely an arbitrary matter, regulated by the quantity of money, or representative of credit, issued by the State.

That what Adam Smith says is absolutely true: "In countries which are fast approaching to riches, the low rate of profit in the price of many commodities, compensate the high wages of labor, and enables those countries to sell as cheap as their less thriving neighbors, among whom the wages paid to labor may be much lower. In reality, high profit tends much more to raise the price of work than high wages."— "Wealth of Nations," book i., chapter ix.

This means, that profit following interest at the top of production is necessarily added into all articles which are manufactured, or go through several processes before fit for final consumption, and that thus a large share of their cost and price is interest and profit. Table vii., appendix hereto, shows that the average of this profit and interest from simple to complex in the United States was, in 1880, over 35 per cent.; that the difference of 1 per cent., therefore, in interest makes from 8 to 18 per cent. in cost, a difference which would break most manufacturers; that England, with an absolute paper money, provided by Peel's act, and France by simple law creating paper money, have it so arranged as to provide for an artificial, arbitrary low interest on money, and could, through the results of this, undersell all outside nations and absorb their raw products, almost all of which is labor (see appendix, table v.), and pay them back in profit and interest, a large share of which is wind and wind duplicated, and thus grow fat on the cream of their labor, and let outsiders grow fat on skimmed milk and wind pudding.

Mr. Mill wrote as an Englishman of his class. If he did not see these truths, he felt them, and wrote political economy from the sense of his feeling. He evidently never borrowed any money. If he had, he would have soon under-

stood that he had not got anything to eat, drink
or wear, but he would find that at regular inter-
vals he would be invited to walk up and deposit
something produced by his labor, to compensate
for the privilege of keeping in his safe this something, which was not giving him anything in return.   He would find if he parted with it, *i. e.*,
the borrowed money, for something which was
capital, with which and his labor, he could produce this compensation, that possibly he could
out of this get enough to pay wear and tear,
wages, and this regular installment of interest.
After a time would come a notice: "Times are
very tight, and we shall be compelled to ask
more interest."   He knew this already in his
slackened demand and fall of profits, etc.; then,
as the interest went up and the profit down, he
would commence to perceive that profit and interest were two different things, and after about
three weeks of walking the floor nights, study-
ing how to make a three-inch auger bore a seven-
inch hole, he would know that interest was not
profit.   The work of Mr. Mill should have been
entitled: "The Science of Political Economy,
Adapted to the Best Interests of the British
Landed and Manufacturing Aristocracy."

Fortunately, time and facts knock the sophisms

out of science. So, if the United States, Mexico, Argentine Republic, or other nations unburdened with aristocratic institutions, can once grasp the magnitude of the questions herein contained, and coin their own credit so as to reduce interest and keep money increasing at such rate as to keep ahead of an increased demand, which any increase always creates, they can send their flax and their hemp, their cotton and iron to the uttermost nations of the earth, not as raw products, but as cheap as they now send raw products, and then pay better wages than now for their production. They can send them in their own iron vessels, and send them direct to China and Japan and the islands of the sea, instead of sending them to England, as we now do, borrowing her cheaper credit to distribute them, because at 6 or 7 per cent. we cannot afford to lay out of the use of the value of the products for six to twelve months.

To send it, as we would now have to do, in vessels, whose cost is recorded in money at 6 to 7 per cent. produced on land, which must produce 6 to 7 per cent. or lose, with implements and freights, and warehouses, and replacement, all to be transacted in credit, which must bring these large interests, creates a difference in re-

sults of from 18 to 30 per cent., and causes a
clear give away of all foreign commerce to nations who construct money on a different basis.

Should these facts once take possession of the
minds of clear-headed representative Americans,
some other John Stuart Mill will be compelled
to write another scientific work, and such statements as the following will constitute a part of it :
"Owing to the fact that the British government
has seen fit to overrule the decrees of divine
providence by demonitizing silver, and, therefore, render it unscientific to call silver money,
I, therefore, yield to the higher power and call
gold, money"   *   *   "Owing to the fact that
wheat and other products of industry are coming into England and breaking down our in-
ternal industry, I am of the opinion that science
is a little wrong in its mind about the protective
tariff."

Time and facts have wrought other wonderful
changes for the better, in men's opinions, on the
powers, duties and privileges of government.
They have rooted out the heresy that liberty
means license; that private greed, or cunning, or
self-interest, shall be permitted to destroy the
source of human happiness, and while we still
write over our portals "that government is the

best which gives the greatest freedom consistent with the public good," we now write the "public good" in large capitals.

Thus, facts, solid and real, have swept from the sky of him who has the vision to see the very coming day dawn, all the black shadows which have obscured the morning of man's deliverance. Those brooding buzzards, the doctrines of Ricardo and Malthus, which have been gnawing at the hearts of men like black despair, accusations against the bounties of that providence, which bedecks every hilltop and sends blessing in every sun's ray, hie themselves to the regions of the damned, and every means to bring equality, justice and human happiness to man, illumine the way, if he is willing to walk therein and partake.

Let men carefully and conscientiously use the means, to correct existing errors which thus present themselves, and all else follows.

The rules which should govern the issue of money are:

1st. It being a function of sovereignty, money should only be issued by the government and not delegated to any individual or corporation.

2nd. It should be a legal tender in the payments of all debts.

3rd. All money by convertibility, exchanga-
bility or security should be made at all times to
represent, and equal in value, the standard of
payment of other nations.

4th. It should be issued in such quantities,
and circulated through banks or public deposi-
tories, as to maintain in all parts of the nation a
uniform interest on the same principles that mail
service is alike for all.

5th. Make the volume to increase in proportion to increased needs, so as to result in an
equation of interest, as near as possible, with the
percentage of advancing wealth.

6th. Make no sudden or violent changes of
currency, but a gradual pressure of money
against business, until it is determined to what
extent production would increase, and, when
found, maintain it there.

The practical details should be left to a bureau,
who should be clothed with power to originate a
scheme by which this, the most important function of government, could be exercised in a manner consistent with an intelligent system to accomplish justice. I shall briefly notice some of
the ways in which money is, has been and can
be made:

1st. Bottomed on taxes, as our greenbacks now are; such money would derive its value from being made a legal tender and from its tax-paying power. Any man who has a tax to pay in gold or its equivalent a piece of paper clothed with power to pay that tax, is equal to gold to him for that occasion. There are seven hundred millions of dollars of taxes to pay each year in the United States, or an absolute gold redemption of seven hundred millions of dollars to redeem three hundred and forty-six millions of dollars of this paper now in circulation. The government keeps up the pleasant fiction of convertability, and keeps a large amount of coin in the treasury, but hardly any of this is ever called for, and fifty thousand dollars would have served this purpose just as well as to have had the vault of the treasury full.

2nd. Coin gold and silver free, but save the expense of coinage by using a certificate issued upon bullion.

I wish to say, by way of parenthesis, that there is but one explanation of the attempt on the part of several leading commercial nations to degrade silver. It is the explanation which this book makes plain. It was the manner taken by that class of people, who always calculate to keep

currency so controlled as to realize high interest, and result in high profit by loan of their
credit. Silver is just as good a metal, more universally esteemed and older in its use as money
than gold. It is far more reliable from these
considerations to maintain an even value than
gold. The object was to decrease the quantity
of money and keep up interest, nothing else. It
was a direct thrust at all silver producing countries and all other production everywhere; an
attempt to increase the power of the non-producing factor of distribution over production. Why,
therefore, a large amount of sycophantish sym-
pathy should be extended to this scheme by
Americans can only be accounted for, on the
grounds that they have more interest in interest
than they have in prosperity and production.
Now that the force of public sentiment has
driven our government in the right direction,
there is a puzzle yet to get back to free coinage
without a shock.

It can be done:

Either by passing a law compelling the secre-
tary of the treasury to coin five or ten millions
of silver more than is produced by the United
States; this would create a demand for foreign
silver, and thus cause silver to go to par—

Or by law compelling the treasury department to advertise for the silver required for each month's coinage on or before the 10th of each month and purchase the same at public or private sale, and thereafter during such months issue certificates upon all bullion which might be offered at the treasury department; such certificates to be issued at the par value of such silver, at the price of such sale, redeemable in standard silver dollars. This would dispose of all silver on the market at this particular price, and the next sale would be higher, and in a short time silver would be at a par with gold.

I believe that the United States can absorb all the silver in the world for sale at its present relative par value with gold, and then, with all the gold added, not make money as fast as it is, and will be demanded by the momentum of our increasing population and business. The people of the United States are fast approaching the condition when they will commence to shut down their factories, and the voice of the tramp will be heard in the land, unless there is an increase of the money of the country faster than any device now provided to this end. Even Mr. Mill says a steady volume of currency is a necessity in any country. The population of the

United States is said to be increasing at the rate
of from 4 to 5 per cent. The money volume is
as much as 50 per cent. behind our present business, and has for four years increased less than
3 per cent. This means a crash.

There is but one trouble about depending
upon silver for money after it goes to par, and
that is, it is the common currency of seven-
tenths of the world, and at par would flow out,
instead of other commodities, to foreign countries, as it always did before the war. It should,
therefore, be coined with a seigniorage, which
would make the coins of more value at home
than abroad, and issue certificates upon gold and
silver at full weight, redeemable in coin. It
would thus in a slight degree, just as much as
the law can interfere with commerce, give a
bonus to ship other commodities, instead of gold
and silver, and thus prevent fluctuation in the
volume of coined money or coin certificates, but
if this failed as silver departed, a paper money
based upon other wealth, which would not be
exported, should be issued so as to keep the
money volume sufficient to meet the demands of
justice.

3rd. The system of land-scrip, which was advocated by Edward Kellogg, might be of use, or

a system based upon mortgages at such a valuation that they would always bring gold or silver par valuation, such as a loan to western farmers at 3 per cent., taking their mortgages as a security for a certificate made full legal tender. These mortgages are now good security to individuals for loans at 10 and 12 per cent. of hundreds of millions of dollars. They would be five times as good security at 3 per cent., and would place the producer on the farm upon something like an equal footing with other classes in society.

4th. Money could be issued upon bonds direct to the people, as it is now issued to national banks.

5th. Money could be issued upon a bond at a low rate of interest, as advocated by a large class of our currency reformers.

6th. I suggest that, as a possible remedy to the existing exactions of combined railroad monopoly, that it may be regulated by the government competing with them at the margin of increasing wealth. As a means of solving two problems in one, the compulsion of the railroads to comply to the laws of justice, and the affording a means of adding a needed currency, I propose that the United States construct a four-

track railroad from the principal eastern cities—
Boston, New York, Philadelphia and Baltimore
—to connect with Chicago, Cincinnati and St.
Louis, and through, by one or two routes, to
San Francisco. That this railroad be paid for
by certificates issued by the United States and
made legal tender for all debts, and that the re-
ceipt of this road, run at a net profit of 2 or 3
per cent., be placed in the treasury as a redemption, or exchange fund, to insure ready convertability to these certificates. That they be exchangeable, if thought best, with a bond bearing
2 or 2½ per cent. interest, issued upon the value
of this road. That power be given to change
the rate of interest upon these bonds from time
to time, as may be necessary to keep them at
par or from appreciating in value. This would
settle the question of freights and railroad traffic
justly, so far as the great bulk of travel and
freights are concerned. A money would be
made, which, in security, convertability and elas-
ticity, would be the acme of all money ever
created upon earth. The system would be su-
perior to the one provided by the act of Peel in
England, in that it always provides its own reserves, and is just as secure in all other respects.

In the same way the exactions of the telegraph may be disposed of.

But why enlarge? Money is now made, and has been made since civilization dawned, out of many things. Mr. Mill says, "Anything is worth whatever can be got for it." Make all money so as much value can be had for it, as the value of the standard adopted as payment, and enough to bar injustice, and then, and not till then, shall come the time, when the thoughtful, the prudent, and industrious, can eat the fruit of their own labor, and the idle and careless shall eat the fruit of their folly.

CONCLUSION.

The law of the universe is immutable and unchangeable. Sequence follows sequence as night follows day. "The soul that sinneth, it shall die," is written in the law of nations, as upon the law which governs individual life ; not as punishment or malediction, but as the natural outcome of cause and effect. The nation that ascribes upon its escutcheon "injustice," or places a barrier against the exercises of equal privileges, writes therein its own epitaph. The power which gives it into the hands of one man, or a class of men, to gather the fruit of other men's labor without adequate return, saps the foundation of self-respect and honor, dries up the fountain of justice and benevolence, and, as a consequence, brings pride of wealth or caste distinctions, based not upon manliness or honor, but rather, on the pride born of arrogance and base ambition; and just as certainly upon him who is despoiled, the ceaseless envy, rancor and

CONCLUSION   217

hatred which debases and benumbs every manly
instinct, and spawns the spirit of foul and loath-
some deeds which walk in darkness, and delight
in blood and revolution.

This is the influence of that potent power we
have outlined, and forms no exception to the
rule. From the dawn of civilization it has exemplified this law. Born with the necessities of
organized society, it has sat upon the throne of
all nations. Nehemiah found it in the vineyard
of the Jews. The day of release, and the year
of jubilee are the shadows which it cast across
Jewish law. Christ found it in the temple. Rome
succumbed as much to it as the Goth or Vandal.
It held sway during the night of the middle
ages, and it has ensconced itself upon modern
civilization. Insidious in its operation, it has
blinded the eyes and benumbed the faculties of
all scientists and thinkers. Through their
errors which I have shown, has entered and
occupied the church, so that the clink of its
gold paralyzes the tongue of the servant of Him
who scourged it from the temple; has conquered
the press; has controlled legislatures; has mis-
directed the energies of the philanthropists, and
warmed beneath the robes of liberty; it gnaws
at the heart of the republic.

And the question of questions which now confronts civilization is, what shall the harvest be? Will the scientist turn from error and teach the truth? Will the pulpit scourge this leprosy from the temple as did the Master? Will public teachers and the press turn from injustice and battle for the rights of all men? Will the vast mass of producers and capitalists who groan under the heat and burden of exactions too grievous for endurance, raise their voices once for wife and child, and equity, and humanity? If so be it that they may, then, and only then, can it be said that the race is born who is fit to unveil its face in the presence of liberty; and if this, the harvest is to be, we stand at the dawn of the brightest day which ever greeted the sleeping eye of seer or sage, or prophet.

No human mind can conceive of the capacity and power of labor to supply the wants, comforts and necessities of life. Everywhere in society men work but a part of the time or stand idle; everywhere in nature, on sea, on land, on hill, and in valleys are idle opportunities inviting them to toil. The city of Chicago, made up of miles and miles of solid stone and iron structures, was laid waste in a single day.

In scarce two years there was built in its place a city far more complete, substantial and attractive. The labor which performed this marvelous feat came mostly from a circuit of one hundred miles, and was scarce missed in other productions. I think a score of such cities could be built in the United States each year and not lessen present production. It could be done by the labor and capital now pinched out from the possibility of using producing opportunities by reason of high interest. This is a crime against production, a crime against labor, a crime against humanity, a crime against civilization. Remove this barrier against production, make the motive to store capital greater than the motive to store money, and all opportunities are at once opened up. The barren hilltops and the dessolate valleys shall teem with verdure, and nurse the vine and shrub laden with blessings. The gleaming sickle shall sing in the golden grain, and the swaying meadows, making melody with the laughter and mirth of the gleamers, and the burden of the song shall be, "No more suffering from want." The sea, and rivers and oceans shall be dotted with white-winged messengers, bearing to every tribe and kindred and tongue, and gathering in return whatever conduces to the happiness and

welfare of men; from the rising of the sun until
the going down thereof, shall be heard the sound
of axe and hammer, fashioning homes in place of
hovel and tenement.

And care shall flee.

And doubt shall flee.

And dread shall flee.

And what are care and doubt and dread? They
are the black sisters who sit and brood and
brood upon the hearts of men and mothers, from
hovel to palace; the children of the parents who
now bar men's labor out from the sunshine and
want and love of God's bounties and blessings.

The parent of the instinct of the miser.

The mother of despair.

As they go, along with justice and plenty, will
come equality; not forced equality, but the
equality of nature; equal returns for equal service; equal rewards for equal culture, capacity
and application; not equality from pulling any-
body down, but by lifting labor up; not by in-
juring or taking anything or any right any other
person possesses, but by establishing justice,
now denied, and granting the right to laboring
men, under the inherent power of the laws of
nature and nature's God, to build themselves up
to an equality with other men.

The banker, then, would receive an equivalent for all the benefit conferred by the use of his money with less liability to loss. The manufacturer would save in the fall of interest, and would be driven by new demand of production to use more capital, and at lower profit would make sufficient to satisfy all rational desire, while the increase of production would go to labor and the producer of raw product, and raise him to an equality with the other factors of production and distribution.

The result of a just return will afford rest and chances for intellectual culture. The reward of high endeavor will quicken mental perception and activity, and multiply and remultiply inventions and devices to facilitate production, until mere getting and accumulation will cease to be the object of the producer. The chief motive for greed and cunning and overreaching will disappear, and the importance and dignity of labor will then be recognized as the beginning and end of all vigorous, intellectual, moral and physical growth; as the source of attainments of that high and manly nobility, which receives nothing without an adequate recompense; aye, of that higher and more glorious walk, to which the spirit of man sometimes ascends, when he is able to realize how much better it is to give than to receive; that earth or heaven has no brighter crown or reward for noble endeavor than the consciousness of deeds done without expectation or hope of reward—of goodness and virtue and benevolence for goodness and virtue's sake.

Out of the record of woe and sorrow, out of the rivers of blood and tears, out of the waiting and sighing and agony, the dead past calls to the present; calls to all men who reverence and love justice; to teachers and thinkers who respect truth; to any and all who can bear a message; by the respect for the wellfare of all you most love; by your hope for the present; by your wish for the future; by the mute appeal of the white lips of the starving; by the voice of pity; by the voice of love, write these truths high upon the scroll of the present; burn them into the consciences and minds of all men, that their light may illumine the pathway of nations and scatter garlands of blessings to the end of the ages.

APPENDIX.

DELUSIONS.

In this work I have attempted, by reasoning from cause to effect, to build up an argument which would carry the reader, by a necessary sequence of acknowledged principles, to absolute, irrefutable conclusions. I have done this, so as to cover just as little ground and just as few facts as possible, and yet make the ideas plain which I wish to convey. In doing this I have left out many statements used in common parlance, which may seem to need explanation. All ordinary conclusions of previous writers must necessarily differ and be erroneous, for the reason I have so often pointed out, and lest some one might be misled by ideas which are constantly met, and which I have not succinctly explained, I shall touch upon the most common of these briefly in one chapter. This will enable the reader, who is unaccustomed to the pursuit of this science, to steer clear of the most common errors which abound in almost every page of the very best writers. They use interchangeable wealth and money, money and gold, confound profit, rent and interest in as many different periods of the same page. They go into an argument, plausible enough, until you observe, they started with interest, talk of it as profit in the middle, and possibly end up with rent.

1st. "Gold is the standard of value."

Error. Nothing is a standard of value. Gold gets its value like beef or lead—fluctuates from same causes, though less than they. All political economists say so without a dissenting voice.

2nd. "Gold is a measure of value"

Wrong again. Nothing is a measure of value, except, possibly, brains. If gold, or money even, was a measure of value, a child could measure the value of any object with a dollar as well as a man. The trouble with this assumption is, that it requires education to enable the person to measure the dollar. No two individuals measure the dollar alike. To one it is a day's work, another one-third or one-tenth of the same; to one it represents wheat, to another cloth, to a child one thing, to a youth another, to a man something different. The average of these educated ideas of the relation of all values ("the money of account"), the idea which is represented by the gold or silver thing we call a dollar, is the nearest a standard of value of anything on earth. This idea is the standard with which we compute all values, even that of the gold in the dollar.

3rd. " Money value is measured by the value of bullion in it."

Wrong again. This was so the first day gold was legalized as money and coined as such; but ever afterwards the value of gold was modified and controlled by its being coined into money. The proper scientific expression is " measure of payment."

4th. " Money of the world."

Is no such thing. The moment money goes out of a country where made, it ceases to be money unless some legal regulation there makes it money or declares its legal status. It is money then, because of such law, and not because it is made of any particular thing.

5th. "To make paper as valuable as gold it must be redeemable in gold or silver."

No political economist of any note says this. Mr. Mill, even, does not pretend but paper can be at par with gold by limitation. The silver certificate is not redeemable in gold, nor anything which is redeemable or exchangeable for gold. It is redeemed in a dollar. This dollar is worth a gold dollar, though it contains but 80 cents worth of silver; the balance of its value is a creation of law. The 80 cents worth of silver is composed of $33\frac{1}{3}$ per cent. profit and interest, and $66\frac{2}{3}$ per cent. labor, so in reality, a silver certificate is redeemable in 53.34 per cent. worth of labor and 26 66 profit and interest, and 20 per cent. of fiat of law.

6th. "If one wants to go to Europe, how can they go there without gold or silver money?"

Nine cases out of ten this question will be asked of any one who advocates paper money in any assembly. The man who asks it is usually one who never went out of his own township unless he walked. But he is always troubled about how to take that trip to Europe, if we should happen to make an equitable supply of paper money. The answer, of course, is to go to a bill broker, buy a bill of exchange, go right over and have a good time. Never on any account take any gold or silver money along. It will not be money there, and you will have to pay quite a discount on it. Besides, if you should happen to be drowned some valuable material would be lost, and if you should happen to go down with a bill of exchange, nothing of any material value would be gone.

7th. " Money is a natural product."

Just as much a natural product and regulated by the law of competition as a legislature, a light-house, a man-of-war or a court of justice.

8th. "Interest is the natural result of competition, and goes up and down with labor; is the result of average profit," as says Mr. George.

In India it is 20 to 50 per cent., in China 15 to 30 per cent. Wages ought to be very high there. That is utterly against all fact. Interest on money is the result of competition for the use of what there is. What there is, is not governed by competition, but by chance, greed, and the want of knowledge of the law of money.

9th. " Gold is real money."

That depends upon whether it is or not. It is, when it is so made by law. Greenbacks made legal tender would be money, or anything else which is a legal tender for debt, and carries the amount of value established by law as the unit or standard of payment. And if it has not this legal power it is not money, though every piece weighs a pound, is pure gold, and studded with diamonds as valuable as those in the coronet of Victoria.

The farmer and laborer says:

"I never borrow money; I care not whether interest is high or low, it does not affect me."

They never eat a loaf of bread but interest is stamped upon its price, and their labor scaled down thereby, nor does the farmer sell beef or a tub of butter, but the price is scaled down by interest, and if, perchance they can pinch and save a little from their earnings, they betake themselves to some banker, where they get three per cent. interest, never thinking that in the victuals they eat and clothing they wear, they consume interest enough each year to pay three per cent. upon the earnings of a life time.

11th. "Inflation."

Never was any such thing. It is the popular bugbear to scare men into paying high prices for credit. No money made to carry the value of the standard of payment ever did or can depreciate until you have an amount far beyond that which I advocate. No man would ever part with such money for less than par, as long as its interest would equal the average increase of wealth.

12th. " Protective tariff protects labor."

Well! Yes and no. The object of protection is to prevent competition in price of foreign goods; that is, to enable home manufacturers to charge an advanced price for products. Now, price is composed of rent, wages, profit and interest. Protection, therefore, is to allow more rent, profit, wages or interest to be charged in price of home products—to protect high rent, profit, interest and wages. Hence, if the rise in price is caused by adding more profit and interest than wages, it would result in a relative decrease of wages. If the relative amount of increase in price was the same from adding profit and interest, and pay of labor, wages would be just the same. So in the sense of increase of wages protective tariff may or may not protect labor. But whether it does or does not increase wages, any people who wish to indulge in the luxury of high interest and consequent high profit, must of a necessity protect them against foreign competition. It is a matter of life and death. As I have shown voluntarily stored capital must make interest on money, or it will be turned into money. The moment such capital (stored for profit) comes in competition with capital stored by money drawing lower interest,

it will cease to compete. 1st. Because it can't
make the interest. 2nd. It has an alternative—
it can do better. The owner of such capital will
gather together his circulating capital and turn
it into credit (loaned money), sell his mills for
junk or let them rot down. His employees
thrown out of employment must stand idle and
starve, or compete with other laborers for a
chance to produce raw products or borrow this
money, store capital, open up land and produce
raw products. This puts interest up and raw
products down. The foreigner buys their cheap
raw products, composed mostly of labor, and
having manufactured them sends them back
burdened with profit and interest, and this duplicated and reduplicated, a large proportion of
which costs nothing (price of credit), and this
nothing, which I have called wind, is a surplus
and must be paid for by some desirable product
of labor. Wages in products exchanged would
equal each other, and this surplus of profit and
interest would constitute a balance against the
home market. Gold and silver must go abroad
to meet this balance of trade; this is a mathematical certainty—must and always does occur
under such circumstances.

This contracts money, raises interest, contracts

production, throws labor out of employment and forces wages lower and lower. Any civilized or half-civilized nation by such a process will be ultimately driven to the lowest state of degradation and misery. Witness India to-day. Capital cannot be coerced to work for low profit so long as it can be turned into credit at high interest. Men only store capital below interest from the pressure of necessity. Under this view a protective tariff is a necessary evil—necessary to all new countries until money is accumulated so as to compete in interest and profit with older nations, or until wisdom, by some divine gift, rests upon the law makers of such people. High interest and consequent high profit are the spikes by which the hands and feet of labor are nailed to the cross of poverty. Protective tariff is an umbrella suspended over it, in the hope that its shade may prolong and perpetuate its travail.

A country like the United States, with a credit equal to England or France, could issue and circulate- her credit as cheap as they, and by making interest in accord with justice, openly compete with any and all nations. The millionaire would become extinct, the laborer raised to the position of independence and manhood, and justice rule and reign.

TABLES COMPILED FROM THE TENTH CENSUS OF
THE UNITED STATES.

———

The following tables are an epitome of facts
drawn from the tenth census of the United States
of America. This census was taken during the
last days of an administration of the government,
which had controlled the affairs of the nation
for twenty years, and was evidently designed to
exhibit the condition of the country in the best
possible light to advance its claims to a continuance of power. It was placed in charge of
the Hon. Francis A. Walker, a man eminently
qualified to give a thorough examination, and to
marshal the results to the best advantage. Am-
ple means were furnished to put special agents
in the field, in departments where no such agents
had been placed before: notably the fisheries,
which had no place in previous returns.

Every effort being thus made to make this
census exhaustive in detail, where any omissions
were found, estimates were added, which esti-

mates, being made by persons interested in giving a full production, may be taken as sufficient
to meet all requirements of truth.   I, therefore,
conclude, that legitimate deductions, from these
returns, and additional estimates, will bear me
out, in being the outside of the quantity of production and cost of distribution of that year.
The main facts were gathered from the census.
All estimates are made by comparison, and study
of these facts—unless otherwise stated.

TABLE I.

Raw products produced in the United States in the year (1879 and 1880) according to the census of 1880, with all additions by estimate:

AGRICULTURAL PRODUCTS.	MEASURE.	QUANTITY.	PRICE.	VALUE.
Corn	Bushels . .	1,754,591,676	39.6	$694,818,304
Wheat	" . .	459,483,137	95.1	436,968,463
Oats	" . .	40⁻,858,999	36.	146,829,240
Rye	" . .	19,831,595	75.6	14,992,686
Barley	" . .	43,997,495	66.6	29,302,332
Buckwheat	" . .	11,817,327	59.4	7,019,492
Rice	Pounds . .	110,131,337	.06	6,607,882
Irish potatoes	Bushels . .	169,458,539	.483	81,848,474
Sweet potatoes . . .	" . .	33,378,693	.45	15,020,412
Hay	Tons . . .	35,150,711	11.65	409,505,783
Cotton	Pounds . .	2,771,797,156	.098	271,636,121
Tobacco	"	472,661,157	.082	38,758,215
Peas and beans . . .	Bushels . .	9,590,027	.150	14,385,041
Market gardening . .	. . . . .	. . . . . .	. . . .	21,761,250
Orchard products . .	. . .	. . . . . .	. . . .	50,876,154
Hops	Pounds . .	26,546,378	.24	6,371,131
Hemp	Tons . . .	5,025	200.00	1,005,000
Flax	Pounds . .	1,565,546	.25	391,387
Flaxseed	Bushels . .	7,170,951	1.25	8,963,689
Cane sugar	Hhds . . .	178,172	90.00	16,098,480
Maple sugar	Pounds .	36,576,061	.13	4,754,888
Cane molasses	Gallons . .	16,573,273	.35	5,800,646
Sorghum syrup . . .	" . .	28,444,202	.33	9,386,587
Maple syrup	" . .	1,796,048	1.00	1,796,048
Beeswax	Pounds . .	1,105,689	.33	364,877
Honey	" . .	25,743,208	.22	5,663,506
Grass seed	Bushels . .	1,317,701	1.50	1,976,552
Cloverseed	" . .	1,922,982	6.00	11,537,892
Wool	Pounds . .	155,681,751	.28	43,590,890
Butter	" . .	777,250,287	.21	163,222,560
Cheese	"	27,272,489	.095	2,590,886
Milk	Gallons . .	530,129,755	.075	39,759,731
Poultry products. . .	. . . . .	. . . . . .	. . .	76,429,309
*Wines	Gallons . .	20,000,000	.60	12,000,000
*Wool product . . .	Pounds . .	85,000,000	.28	a 23,800,000
*Meat	. . . . .	. . . . . .	. . .	c800,000,000
*Butter	Pounds . .	122,749,713	.21	b 25,777,440
*Cheese	"	272,727,511	.095	b 25,909,114
*Milk	Gallons . .	1,269,870,245	.075	95,240,269
*Poultry	. . . . .	. . . . . .	. . . .	103,570,691

Total agricultural products $3,726,331,422

*Estimated by the Hon. J. R. Dodge, Commissioner of Agriculture.

NON-PRECIOUS METALS.

Anthracite coal . . .	Tons . . .	28,698,812	. . . .	$ 42,196,678
Bituminus coal . . .	'' . . .	41,860,055	. . . .	52,427,869
" irr. mines.	" . . .	916,569	. . . .	1,092,305
Iron ore	. . . . .	7,974,706	. . . .	23,156,957
Copper, lead, zinc and others	. . . . . .	. . . . . .	. . . .	25,021,024

Total non-precious metals $143,894,832

Total precious metals, gold and silver $74,490,620

FORESTRY.

Wood, domestic use.	. . . . . .	. . . . . .	. . . .	$306,950,040
Saw logs	. . . . . .	. . . . . .	. . . .	139,832,869
Sundries.	. . . . . .	. . . . . .	. . . .	43,290,185
Estimated by Commissioner of Forrestry	. . . . . .	. . . . . .	. . . .	100,000,000

Total of forestry $590,073,094

Petroleum	Barrels . .	24,235,081	.90	20,411,572
Quarries, total	. . . . . .	. . . . . .	. . . .	18,356,058
Fisheries, total . . .	. . . . . .	. . . . . .	. . . .	43,046,053

Grand total all raw products $4.616.603,651

"a." 34,000,000 pounds wool from ranches, not from farms, 28 cents, $9,520,000.

"b." This cheese and butter contain a part of milk sold to butter and cheese factories (530,129,755 gallons), to wit: 312,702,666 at 07.5 per gallon=$23,415,574, a clean duplicate.

"c." A part of this meat is produced on ranches and part in towns and villages, estimated to 2.6 per cent. of the total product of corn, which amount is sold outside for this purpose.

TABLE II.

DISPOSITION OF RAW PRODUCTS, RETURNED BY THE 10TH
   CENSUS OF THE UNITED STATES OF AMERICA, AND
   ESTIMATED OMISSIONS, YEAR 1879–80; WITH A VIEW
   OF SHOWING FARMING, MANUFACTURING AND MIN-
   ING PROFITS AND PER CENT OF PROFITS.

RAW PRODUCTS.	CONSUMED ON THE FARM.		
		PRICE.	AMOUNT OF SEED.
Corn	Bushels.	$ .39.6	15,592,123
Wheat	"	.95.1	62,003,082
Oats	"	.36	40,361,486
Rye	"	.75.6	2,763,349
Barley	"	.66.6	3,995,454
Buckwheat	"	.59.4	848,389
Rice	Pounds.	.06	10,450,380
Irish Potatoes	Bushels.	.48.3	15,062,976
Sweet Potatoes	"	.45	. . . . . .
Hay	Tons.	11.65	. . . . . .
Cotton	Pounds.	.09.8	. . . . . .
Peas and Beans	Bushels.	1.50	. . . . . .
Market Garden	. . . . .	. . . .	. . . . . .
Orchard Products	. . . . .	. .24	. . . . . .
Hops	Pounds.	.24	. . . . . .
Hemp	Tons.	200.00	. . . . . .
Flax	Pounds.	.25	. . . . . .
Flax Seed	Bushels.	1.25	717,095
Cane Sugar	Hogsh'ds	.90	. . . . . .
Maple Sugar	Pounds.	.13	. . . . . .
Tobacco	"	.08.2	. . . . . .
Cane Molasses	Gallons.	.35	. . . . . .
Sorghum	"	.33	. . . . . .
Maple Syrup	"	1.00	. . . . . .
Beeswax	Pounds.	.33	. . . . . .
Honey	"	.22	. . . . . .
Grass Seed	Bushels.	1.50	1,185,931
Clover Seed	"	6.00	1,480,878
Wines	Gallons.	.60	. . . . .
Wool	Pounds.	.28	e
Meat c	. . . . .	. . . . .	e
Butter	Pounds.	.21	e
Cheese	"	.09.5	e
Milk	Gallons.	.07.5	e
Poultry	. . . . .	. . . . .	e
Total of			Seed.

TABLE II.—CONTINUED.

	CONSUMED ON THE FARM.			
DOLLARS.	WORK ANIMALS. AMOUNT.	DOLLARS.	MEAT AND MILK PRODUCT.	DOLLARS.
6,174,698	491,285,669	194,549,125	756,428,214	299,545,355
58,964,931	. . .	. . . . . .	. . . . . .	. . . . . .
14,530,133	203,929,499	73,414,620	. . . . . .	. . . . . .
2,089,092	. . . . . .	. . . . . .	. . . . . .	. . . . . .
2,660,972	. . . . . .	. . . . . .	. . . . . .	. . . . . .
503,943	. . . . . .	. . . . . .	. . . . . .	. . . . . .
627,022	. . . . . .	. . . . . .	. . . . . .	. . . . . .
7,275,417	. . . . . .	. . . . . .	. . . . . .	. . . . . .
. . . . . .	13,164,137	. . . . . .	12,443,120	144,962,348
. . . . . .	. . . . . .	153,362,196	. . . . . .	. . . . . .
. . . . . .	. . . . . .	. . . . . .	. . . . . .	. . . . . .
. . . . . .	. . . . . .	. . . . . .	. . . . . .	. . . . . .
. . . . . .	. . . . . .	. . . . . .	. . . . . .	. . . . . .
. . . . . .	. . . . . .	. . . . . .	. . . . . .	. . . . . .
896,368	. . . . . .	. . . . . .	. . . . . .	. . . . . .
. . . . . .	. . . . . .	. . . . . .	. . . . . .	. . . . . .
. . . . . .	. . . . . .	. . . . . .	. . . . . .	. . . . . .
. . . . . .	. . . . . .	. . . . . .	. . . . . .	. . . . . .
. . . . . .	. . . . . .	. . . . . .	. . . . . .	. . . . . .
. . . . . .	. . . . . .	. . . . . .	. . . . . .	. . . . . .
. . . . . .	. . . . . .	. . . . . .	. . . . . .	. . . . . .
1,778,897	. . . . . .	. . . . . .	. . . . . .	. . . . . .
8,885,268	. . . . . .	. . . . . .	. . . . . .	. . . . . .
. . . . . .	. . . . . .	. . . . . .	. . . . . .	. . . . . .
. . . . . .	. . . . . .	. . . . . .	. . . . . .	. . . . . .
. . . . . .	. . . . . .	. . . . . .	. . . . . .	. . . . . .
. . . . . .	. . . . . .	. . . . . .	. . . . . .	. . . . . .
. . . . . .	. . . . . .	. . . . . .	. . . . . .	. . . . . .
104,386,741	Fed work animals.	421,325,941	Fed Cows, Hogs and Cattle.	144,962,348 299,545,355

TABLE II.—CONTINUED.

CONSUMED ON THE FARM		TRANSPORTED FROM FARM.		
HUMAN FOOD AMOUNT.	DOLLARS.	FED MEAT PRODUCING ANIMALS.	DOLLARS.	CONSUMPT'N RAW. AMOUNT.
140,367,334	55,585,464	a 45,619,383	18,065,275	. . . . . .
. . .	. . . . . .	. . . . . .	. . . . . .	81,400,826
. . . . . .	. . . . . .	. . . . . .	. . . . . .	. . . . . .
. . . . . .	. . . . . .	. . . . . .	. . . . . .	. . . . . .
. . . . . .	. . . . . .	. . . . . .	. . . . . .	89,230,613
77,197,781	37,286,528	. . . . . .	. . . . . .	74,697,784
16,689,346	7,510,206	. . . . . .	. . . . . .	16,689,346
. . . . . .	. . . . . .	. . . . . .	. . . . . .	9,543,454
. . . . . .	. . . . . .	. . . . . .	. . . . . .	. . . . . .
4,795,014	7,192,521	. . . . . .	. . . . . .	4,795,013
. . . . . .	. . . . . .	. . . . . .	. . . . . .	. . . . . .
. . . . . .	23,024,534	. . . . . .	. . . . . .	. . . . . .
. . . . . .	. . . . . .	. . . . . .	. . . . . .	. . . . . .
. . . . . .	. . . . . .	. . . . . .	. . . . . .	. . . . . .
. . . . . .	. . . . . .	. . . . . .	. . . . . .	. . . . . .
. . . . . .	. . . . . .	. . . . . .	. . . . . .	. . . . . .
18,288,031	2,377,444	. . . . . .	. . . . . .	18,288,031
. . . . . .	. . . . . .	. . . . . .	. . . . . .	. . . . . .
. . . . . .	6,257,724	. . . . . .	. . . . . .	. . . . . .
18,962,802	898,324	. . . . . .	. . . . . .	9,481,401
898,324	. . . . . .	. . . . . .	. . . . . .	898,320
. . . . . .	2,265,402	. . . . . .	. . . . . .	. . . . . .
10,297,282	. . . . . .	. . . . . .	. . . . . .	15,445,923
. . . . . .	. . . . . .	. . . . . .	. . . . . .	131,770
. . . . . .	1,200,000	. . . . . .	. . . . . .	. . . . . .
2,000,000	. . . . . .	. . . . . .	. . . . . .	18,000,000
. . . . . .	182,868,364	. . . . . .	. . . . . .	. . . . . .
. . . . . .	72,304,120	. . . . . .	. . . . . .	. . . . . .
344,305,336	. . . . . .	. . . . . .	. . . . . .	516,458,004
68,978,431	6,552,952	. . . . . .	. . . . . .	. . . . . .
720,000,000	54,000,000	. . . . . .	. . . . . .	103,467,656
. . . . . .	72,000,000	. . . . . .	. . . . . .	767,792,335

TABLE II —CONTINUED.

| FORESTS, LAKES AND MINES. | | | MANUFACTURED. | |
DOLLARS.	EXPORT RAW. AMOUNT.	DOLLARS.	AMOUNT.	DOLLARS.
	98,169,877		347,496,409	137,608,577
	153,252,795		304,775,737	289,841,735
29,304,297	766,366		81,400,826	29,304,297
	2,912,754		14,155,492	10,701,552
	1,128,923		39,873,118	25,889,498
			10,968,938	6,515,549
5,353,837			10,450,380	627,022
36,075,028			2,500,000	1,207,500
7,510,206				
111,181,239				
	1,628,372,833	159,580,537	1,143,424,323	112,055,583
7,192,520				
20,018,611				1,742,639
13,370,780		2,403,543		12,051,297
	5,458,159	1,309,958	21,088,219	5,061,173
			5,025	1,005,000
			1,565,546	391,387
			6,453,956	8,067,332
			178,812	16,098,480
2,377,444				
	215,910,187	17,704,735	207,149,754	16,986,280
			16,573,273	5,800,646
3,128,862				
898,320				
			1,105,689	364,877
3 598,103				
197,655				
	442,104	2,652,624		
10,800,000				
	191,551	53,634		
274,302,546		15,882,120	240,490,200	67,337,256
108,456,180	39,236,658	8,239,698		326,946,960
9,829,420	127,553,907	12,117,621		
57,584,426			b 312,207,665	23,415,574
108,000,000				
				1,099,020,214

TABLE II.—CONTINUED.

	FOREST AND MINES.		MANUFACTURED.	
	AMOUNT.	DOLLARS.	AMOUNT.	DOLLARS.
NON-PRECIOUS MET'LS				
Anthricite Coal . . .	. . . . .	25,816,377	1,362,901	15,017,397
Bituminous	. . . . .	26,422,150	695,181	25,310,530
Irregular Mines . . .	436,92c	655,383	. . . . .	. . . . .
Iron Ore	. . . . .	. . . . . .	. . . .	23,156,957
Copper, lead, zinc etc.	. . . . .	. . . . . .	. . . .	25,021,024
Total, ...	. . . . .	. . . .	. . . .	88,505,908
PRECIOUS METALS				
Gold and Silver . . .	. . . . .	. . . . . .	. . . .	27,245,310
FOREST PRODUCT.				
Wood, Logs, etc. . . d	95,774,735	211,175,305	. . . . .	283,123,054
Petroleum	. . . . .	. . . . .	1,192,220	19,219,343
Fisheries, ...	. . . .	43,046,053	. . . .	
Quarries	. . . . .	. . . . . .	. . . .	18,356,058
Total products, raw .	. . . . .	. . . . . .	. . . .	1,535,469,890
Imports, manufactured	. . . . .	. . . . . .	. . . .	386,632,648
Add ¼ R.R. ft. charg's	. . . . .	. . . . . .	. . . .	104,086,439
" ¼ freight on water.	. . . . .	. . . . . .	. . . .	40,096,247
" ¾ canal freights .	. . . . .	. . . . . .	. . . .	1,134.655
Total Imports & Ft's.	. . . . .	. . . . .	. . . .	531,899.989
Total of all Products, entering into manufacture, freight ad'd.	. . . . .	. . . . . .	. . . .	$ 2,067,369,879

a. Transported off of the farm and fed to produce meat in the towns.

b. Part of milk reported in farm products and charged to agriculture as milk.

c. Part made on ranches and off of the farm in towns and villages.

d. One hundred million added by estimate of commissioner for omissions.

e. Hon. J. R. Dodge, commissioner of agriculture, adds by estimate 1,086,297.514 to these items to make the grand total of agricultural production 3,726,331,422. Transportation charged in proportion to total products transported.

All estimates made on returns in census, except, perhaps, 10 per cent., and such, when there is a doubt, are taken against the claims sought to be established; and when it is seen that a mistake of ten millions makes but one-one thousandth of 1 per cent. in my calculations, it will not be questioned that they are accurate beyond any necessity.

TABLE III.

SHOWING CONDITION OF THE FARMER:

Charge farm with agricultural products $3,726,331,422
"   "   "   wood consumed and sold   95,774,735

Total $3,822,106,157

CREDIT FARM WITH

2.6. of corn fed to meat producing animals
  off of farm . . . . $ 18,065,275
Corn fed to work animals on farm (see table ii.) 194,549,172
Oats "   "   "   "   "   "   73,414,620
Hay "   "   "   "   "   "   153,362,196
Hay "   "   milch cows "   "   144,962,348
Wool charged to agricultural products grown
  on ranch (see table ii) 9,520,000
Milk sold to manufacturers (charged twice,
  see table ii) 23,415,574
Seed (see table ii.) 104,386,741   721,675,879

Total sold off farm, chargeable to farmer. $3,100,430,278

CREDIT CONTINUED.

Wages of 620,729 boys, $6.00 per month (board) $44,692,488
"   458,648 women, $13 per month (4
  board and 2 per week) 71,549,088
Wages of 2,583,116 men, $21 per month (12
  board and 9) 649,945,708
By expense, fences 77,763,473
"   "   manures 28,586,397
By taxes 71.6 per cent. of assessment 223,929,516
Replacement stock, 10 per cent. 190,698,466
2 per cent. profits on assessed valuation . . . 242,081,628   1,529,246,178

Divisible as wages to 4,008,907 farmers . . $1,571,184,100
Which equals for 300 days $391.92 or $1.30½ per day.

This table is made on the basis of the census of 1880. I charge the farmer with all agricultural products as returned in the census and also with $1,086,297,514, which Hon. J. R. Dodge estimates was omitted by the census; also $95,774,735 wood consumed by farmers. I credit him with wool grown on ranches and butter and cheese twice charged as milk sold to cheese factories and afterwards estimated as butter; 2.6 per cent. of corn is estimated to have been fed off the farm to meat products charged him, and hence is a duplicate. I deduct this. I deduct wages paid to boys $6.00 per month, women $13.00 and men $21.00 ($12 and board). These cover all wages, except those of the farmer himself, for threshing, cutting, seeding and hauling grain to market. I allow him $32.00 to feed a work horse one year, or 2.4 cents worth of corn and 3.3 cents worth of hay per day at the schedule price.   For replacement of a horse I allow $5.40 each year, and for use he gets $1.08 and nothing for shoeing.

I allow nothing for salt, repairs of barn or house, insurance, or interest on the mortgage.   He must take care of all of these out of his profit of $60 38 on his $391.92 of wages, as well as feed, clothe and educate a family of five.

Each farm averages in whole numbers 134 acres at $19 per acre or $2,544, and at 2 per cent. brings the farm $50.88, two-thirds of which may be termed rent.   He gets at same rate 2 per cent. on $475 of capital in his stock and machinery, or $9.50 each year.

TABLE IV.

SHOWING CONDITION OF THE MANUFACTURER.

Total sales of all manufacturers		$5,369,579,191
Total raw products used	$2,067,369,879	
Duplications and repurchases	1,329,453,670	
Total materials show by census . . .	$3,396,823,549	
Wages paid	947,943,795	4,344,777,344
Total to profit, interest and incidentals		$1,025,801,847
I estimate these incidentals to be:		
Taxes, 14.12 per cent. of all taxes	44,204.222	
¼ of all insurance	14,661,046	
⅓ of all postage	12,180,936	
⅓ of all telegraph cost	5,565,577	
½ of all telephone cost	1,098,081	
⅓ of all paper manufactured	18,336,637	
1-6 of all publishing	10,089,083	
10 per cent. replacement, working capital,		
½ total capital	139,513,630	245,649,219
Balance for profit, loss and interest . .		$780,152,628
Total wages paid	$947,953,795	

Of this 181,921 children get 45 cents per day or $24,559,335; 531,639 women get 75 cents per day, $119,618,775, and the balance is divided between 2,019,035 males, who get $396.86 per year or $1.32¼ per day. The census shows that materials were purchased and used in manufacturing to the amount of $3,396,823,549, and that it sold for $5,369,-579,191. The most casual observation shows that a large amount of these purchases were repurchases of the same material in different stages and processes of manufacture.

Iron appears as ore, as steel, as springs, as wire, as watch springs. From table ii. I get the total (and I think I estimate it high), which goes raw to manufactories, as $2,069,369,879, and this is bought and portions rebought, until with profits and wages added, it sells for $5,369,579,191. Computed over and over again it adds to the price the compounded profits, but not necessarily in the same ratio to manufacturers' profits.

I have credited the manufacturer with the most liberal estimate of all incidentals which enter into expenses, and class the balance as profit, loss and interest, or added expense to cost. For profit in manufactured goods see table v.

TABLE V.

Percentage of profit and interest which is found in price of agricultural products.

	P. AND I.	TOTALS.	WAGES.	
Gross total sold from farms	. . . . .	$766,186,708	. . . . .	$3,100,430,288
This total is composed of farm laborers' wages. (This wages is composed of board, $351,687,896; One-half of this is manufactured goods, groceries; etc. or $175,598,586)	. . . . .		. . . . .	. . . . .
One-third of this is profit and interest	$58,531,316	58,531,316	707,655,392	. . . . .
Fences, total		77,763,474		. . . . .
25 per cent. profit and interest in fences (mostly manufactured goods	19,440,868	19,440,868	58,322,605	. . . . .
Manures		28,586,397	19,057,598	. . . . .
33⅓ per cent. equals profit and interest	9,528,799	9,528,799		. . . . .
Taxes		223,929,516		. . . . .
Interest to say nothing of profit (probably much more	52,995,996	52,995,996	170,973,520	. . . . .
Replacement of capital, 10 per cent		190,698,466		. . . . .
33⅓ per cent. profit in replacement of machinery .	16,260,800	16,260,800	174,437,666	. . . . .
Wages of farmer			1,571,184,100	. . . . .
Profit and rent 2 per cent	242,081,628			. . . . .
Or a total of 12.9 per cent. of profit in agricultural products and 87.1 per cent. of wages or labor . .	$398,799,507	. . . . .	$2,701,630,881	$3,100,430,278

In calculating profit and interest two things must always be kept in mind :

1st. That the percentage of profit and of interest paid by the manufacturer and the percentage of profit and interest which appear in the goods are entirely different things. Thus capital, $10,000, produces $4,000; gets profit, $1,000. He has made 10 per cent. on capital. but to do so has charged in price 25 per cent., which is added to goods, and if he paid $1,000 of interest, the goods would stand 50 per cent. profit, interest and 50 per cent. wages.

2nd. All expenses, such as coal, oil, stock, repairs, etc., are constituted partly of labor and partly of previous profit and interest added to goods. Take the railroad as an example. All freights go into things transported as cost. Gross earnings in round numbers, $661,000,000. net, $225,000,000. The $225,000,000 (34 per cent. of total amount) is charged up on cost of goods. This same amount only represents 3 per cent. plus of dividends and about 7 per cent. of interest on stocks and bonds. This is a superficial showing; add to the side of profit and interest profit which had already been charged upon taxes, oils, coals, etc., and it appears as 43 per cent. in the goods. I have put in only patent profit and interest in my calculations, and in all cases where there was doubt kept under the truth, as this goes against my theory and gives no cause for cavil. All valuable railroad stocks are more or less watered. If this was left out and profit and interest computed by actual cost, it would show that 60 to 70 per cent. of receipts charged up as cost on goods transported is profit and interest.

TABLE VI.

Percentage of profit and interest which appears in price of articles which enter into manufacturing.

	P. AND I.	TOTALS.	WAGES.	GROSS TOTALS.
Gross total of all articles manufactured				$2,067,369,879
Total agricultural products—P. and I. 12 9 per cent. and wages 87.1 per cent.—from table v. and ii.	$141,773,607	$1,099,020,214	957,246,607	
Non-precious metals ..		88,505,908	55,957,733	
" 36.8 per cent. profit and interest	32,548,175	32,548,175		
Precious metals		27,245,310	17,182,273	
" profit and interest 36.8 per cent.	10,063,037	10,063 037		
Forestry, total ..		283,123,054	226,493,444	
" profit and interest estimated 20 per cent.	56,624,610	56,624,610		
Petroleum		19,219,343	12,812,896	
" profit and interest 33.6 per cent.	6,406,447	6,406,447		
Imports		386,632,648	309,306,119	
" profit and interest estimated 20 per cent	77,326,529	77,326,529		
Quarries ..		18,356,058	11,601,029	
" profit and interest 33⅓ per cent.	6,755,029	6,755,029		
⅓ of all railroad freights ..		104,036,439	59,300,771	
" profit and int. 43 per cent	44,735,668	44,735,668		
⅓ of all steam and sail freights		40,096,247	22,854,848	
" profit and int. 43 p. c.	17,241,399	17,241,399		
⅓ of all canal freights		1,134,655	646,754	
" profit and interest	487,901	487,901		
Totals, = Wages 81 per cent. --, and profit and interest=19 per cent. plus	$393,962,402		$1,673,407,474	$2,067,369,879

TABLE VII.

Showing per cent. of profit and interest in manufactured goods to final delivery :

	P. and I.	Wages.	P. and I.	Total.	Wages.
Total sales of all m'f'rs . 5,369,519,191					
Raw product bought . . . 2,067,369,879					
Duplications, repurchases 1,329,453,670 3,396,823,549					
Total to profit, interest, wages and incidentals 1,972,755,642					
Raw products bought (see table vi.)			393,962,402	2,067,369,879	1,673,407,474
Manufacturers' wages are					947,953,797
Profit, interest and incidentals, 14.12 per cent of					
taxes, 25 per cent. profit and interest	11,051,055	33,153,167			
¼ insurance, 25 per cent. profit and interest	3,665,261	10,995,785			
⅓ of all postage, 25 per cent. profit and interest	3,045,234	9,135,702			
⅓ of all telegraph receipts, 40 per cent. prof. & int.	2,226,230	3,339,347			
½ of all telephone receipts, 25 per cent. prof. & int.	274,550	823,261			
33⅓ of all paper supplies. 33⅓ per cent prof. & int.	6,112,212	12,224,426			
1-6 of all advertising, 33 per cent. prof. & int.	3,263,027	6,726,056			
1-6 replacement, avearge profit and interest	46,504,543	93,009,087			
Total profit, interest and wages in incidentals			76,242,081	245,649,219	169,407,131
Credit balance of profit and interest (table iv.)			780,152,628		
Totals without profits in repurchases			1,250,357,112		2,790,768,400
This gives as total manufactured productions, 4,041,125,515, all this is composed of profit, 31 per cent., and wages 69 per cent.; add this 31 per cent. profit on repurchases a			412,139,637		
Which gives as total product, 4,453,256,149			1,662,487,749	4,453,256,149	2,790,768,400
Which is composed of 37 per cent. pluss pro. & int. and bal. wages; add balance of transportation			62,464,968	145,269,341	82,804,373
Total production delivered to customers less per cent. of middle man, 37.5 per cent. P. & I.			1,724,952,717	4,598,525,490	2,873,573,773

TABLE VII.—CONTINUED.

To show how this figures up, I append this proposition, figured out in millions. Starting with 2067 and reselling 3 times, these goods, adding, first 24 wages and 26 profit, next 29 and 31, lastly 41 & 43.

Thus:

```
        81*   19*   24*    26*     68*      32*      68*       32*          68*      32*
2067=(1674-|-393)-|-(496-|-537)=3100=(2160-|-931)=2300=(1564-|-736)-|-800=(544-|-256)
                     68*    32*             60†      40†
 800=( 554-|-256)-|-(232-|-248)=1200=(786-|-504)-|- 751=( 450-|-301)-|-259=(317-|-212)
        60†   40†   41†    45†            54†      47†
 529=( 317-|-212)-|-(216-|-238)= 983=(533-|-450)
3396              944-|-1023 = 5363=3488-|-1865
```

* † Per cent.

Thus 2,067 represents the millions which above appear as bought by manufacturers. It is composed of 81 per cent. wages and 19 per cent. profit and interest. Add by manufacturing $1,633 in the proportion of 24 per cent. wages and 26 per cent. profit and interest and we have cost of $3300; by adding wages to wages and (P. and I.) to (P. and I.) in this it amounts to 68 per cent. wages and 32 per cent. profit. Now, resell $800, adding $480 in proportion of 29 to 31 per cent., and again $329, adding $454 in proportion of 41 to 45 per cent. By adding all sales and resales, wages (P. and I.), it results in about the condition above shown by the census, to wit: Purchases and repurchases, $8,396 millions; wages, $944 millions; (P. and I.) $1,023 millions; total value, $5,363 millions. Thus, when the products have gone through three purchases and repurchases, so as to meet the conditions of census, profit, etc., has gone up from 19 to 35 per cent., and there is hid in this transaction $412,630,137 of profit and interest which comes out of the purchaser by compounding (P. and I.)

TABLE VIII.

Showing production of the United States for 1880, as census estimates:

Total raw products	4,616,603,651	. . . . . .	
Amount manufactured	2,067,369,879	. . . . .	
Balance consumed raw or exported . . .	. . . . . .	2,549,233,772	
One-half R. R. freight charges delivering this	. . . .	290.538,682	
Total value of manufactured goods (duplication omitted)	. . . . . .	4,598,525,490	
Paid middle men for rehandling and distribution, 20 per cent.	. . . . . .	948,818,966	
Total gross production (everything added	. . . . . .	8,387,116,910	
Total working capital reported 11,451,225,619, one-half of which is stored by money and pays int. at about an average of 7 per cent.	400,892,896	. . . . . .	
Ten per cent. replacement on balance (waste)	572,561,280	. . . . . .	
Fed to work-animals and cows	669,675,026	. . . . . .	
National taxes	333,526,610	. . . . . .	
State, county and municipal taxes	312,750,721	. . . . . .	
Postage	36,542,804	. . . . . .	
Insurance	90,699,234	. . . . . .	
After taking out all necessary incidentals, but no profit or duplicate interest . . .	. . . . . .	5,970,568,339	
Wages of boys engaged in manufacturing . .	24,559,335	. . . . . .	
Wages of women engaged in manufacturing	119,618,775	. . . . . .	
Wages of boys engaged in farming	44,692,488	. . . . . .	
Wages of women engaged in farming	71,047,800	. . . . . .	
All other boys, women and old men not in personal or professional service	71,047,800	. . . . . .	
In professional service, boys at board $6 per month	29,670,264	. . . . . .	
In professional service, women at board at $13 per month	189,569,487	550,707,234	
Total balance to be divided	. . . . . .	5,419,861,105	

Total professionals and other laborers, 12,986,111. which gives to each $417.28 per year, or $1.39 per day.

Thus, if all the production of 1880 was equally divided between professional and wage working laborers, they could only each get $417.28 per year of 300 days, or $1.39 per day.

If we divide this total production between wage workers alone and allow that they support the professionals, it would be divided by 10,539,149 and give per year of 300 days to each $523.76, or per day $1.74½.

It is not in reality so divided. By examining table iii. it will be seen that farmers get $391.92 or $25.36 less than this; farm laborers get $240, or $177.28 less than this; mechanics get (table iv.) $20.24 less than this; miners get $76.26 less than this.

By multiplying these amounts by the amounts of laborers in each branch respectively, it will be found that it amounts to $613,008,186, which sum is pinched out of all labor by high interest and profits to pay the same. The balance of profit and interest is collected, as I have shown, by adding to goods (an average of 20 per cent. upon all manufactured goods) and equals $979,705,198, about one-half of which comes out of farmers and the balance out of the remainder of society.

It is thus not hard to see where the millionaires come from.

The 20 per cent. profit and interest on manufactured goods takes enough out of the farmer to absorb all the profit of his land and capital (rent and profit) and make 240 millionaires besides.

The interest and profit out of the balance to make 480 millionaires, or 960 half millionaires. The railroads alone absorb to pay interest, nearly twice as much as their capital averages to make, all of which goes in the same way.